DEVELOPING CITIZENSHIP IN SECONDARY SCHOOLS

A WHOLE-SCHOOL RESOURCE

David Turner and Patricia Baker

KOGAN PAGE

First published in 2000 by Kogan Page Limited

Kogan Page Limited
120 Pentonville Road
London N1 9JN
UK

British Library Cataloguing in Publication Data

A CIP record for this book is available from the British Library.

ISBN 0 7494 33469

Typeset by D & N Publishing, Hungerford, Berkshire
Printed and bound in Great Britain by Thanet Press Ltd, Margate

DEVELOPING CITIZENSHIP IN SECONDARY SCHOOLS

CONTENTS

ACKNOWLEDGEMENTS

David Turner and Patricia Baker wish to express their heartfelt thanks to all the people who contributed ideas and materials for use in this book. The list is a long one and includes a large number of the staff at Wellsway School. They are:

Paul Kent (Head Teacher) for allowing the project to go ahead in the school and for making invaluable suggestions about how the task could be managed without the additional burden becoming too overwhelming.

Special thanks to Clarissa Moncrieff (English Teacher), who not only contributed English and PSHE lessons but also took a keen interest in the book and made a number of valuable suggestions.

Jan Barrett (Assistant Head Teacher) for allowing her work on the school council to be used in Chapter 3 and for her generosity with her time.

Greg Price (Assistant Head Teacher) for his help with the section on the election of school officers.

Jill Stanley (Professional Assistant, Development and Training) for her support and co-authorship of the chapters on a school festival/activities week and running a charity event.

Neil Patterson (sixth-form student and organizer of the fashion show) for contributing his time and sharing information to allow Chapter 6 to be written.

Guy Martin (Drama/English Teacher and the author of Chapter 7), who shared his expertise in managing public debate, and with John Smith (Drama Teacher) contributed their work on theatre as a medium for education.

Linda Hall (Head of Philosophy and belief and the author of Chapter 8) for sharing her experience of running a subject-specific day for a large number of pupils.

Dave Sage (Head of Biology), who contributed Chapter 9 and the lesson on noise and whose commitment to environmental action contributes so much to the area of citizenship.

Kim Humphreys (sixth-form student and inspiration behind the Buddy System) who willingly spent time explaining the concept and allowing us to use her work as the basis for Chapter 10.

Max Harvey (Head of Drama) who wrote the section on the school production.

Debbie Barker (PE Teacher) for generously giving time to explain the rationale behind and organization of the Evening of Dance and for allowing us to use her work in Chapter 11.

Anna Barker (Key Skills Co-ordinator) for her suggestions around key skills.

Elaine Holmes (Assistant, Personnel, Development and Training) for her invaluable word-processing skills.

Karen Frost (Geography Teacher) for her lesson on shanty towns.

Roy Lofkin (Head of Modern Languages) for his German lesson looking at rights and responsibilities for young people.

Roy Page (Music Teacher) for his lesson on rhythms.

Shaun Wainwright (Core Technology Co-ordinator) for his lessons on technology and the quality of life.

Allan Baird (Wellsway School and University of Bath novice teacher) for his lesson on house prices and percentages.

Without their help and assistance, freely and willingly given, this book would never have seen the light of day.

Lastly special thanks must go to Peter Baker, Patricia's husband, who acted as a critical friend and who had to put the children to bed far more often than was, strictly, his turn and to Poppy Turner, David's wife, whose original idea this was and who spent a lot of time copy typing and proofing and keeping the project on track.

PREFACE

The recent introduction of the concept of citizenship into schools is no great innovation to many teachers who are already addressing similar issues on a daily basis or during tutor group and PSHE lessons. However, the concept has now been more clearly defined and many teachers will find themselves faced with having to deliver lessons on and around the citizenship agenda for the first time.

This book is intended to be a dip-in resource for school managers and teachers at Key Stages 3 and 4. It is hoped that it will be useful both as a source of ready-made relevant material and as a thought-promoter. Many of the activities in the book can be amended and extended in a variety of different ways and the methods suggested can be adapted for use with different content.

The book is one of two that are intended to be stand-alone resources. This first volume is addressed to the management team of a school who wish to provide widescale opportunities for learning in the citizenship arena within the whole school or larger (eg whole-year) groups. The second book, *Activities for Teaching Citizenship in Secondary Schools*, is aimed at the classroom teacher who will have to teach citizenship issues, either in PSHE classes or in mainstream curriculum lessons. The two books together provide a flexible and easily accessible source of ideas for use in a wide range of situations.

The books are the result of a collaboration between an independent management consultant, David Turner, who is the author of a book of role play resources for management trainers, and members of the teaching staff at Wellsway School in Keynsham, near Bristol, led by Patricia Baker, the Deputy Head Teacher at the school. The material presented here is either directly derived from activities already tried and tested in the school or developed for the purpose and classroom-tested for the books.

In common with many schools, Wellsway is adamant that there is no need to respond to every new initiative by setting up complex structures and new working parties. Enough demands are placed upon education and educators without the profession adding more to the workload. Thus, when some new requirement comes over the horizon, the first response is to see what is already being done in that area under some other guise.

At Wellsway, after having looked at the guidelines for citizenship, we felt pretty confident that we had some good things already going on in that area. Many other schools must also feel this and sharing good practice between schools is important. It not only spreads examples of 'things which work' but also cuts down on the workload of colleagues. As a school we wanted to share our expertise and we are also grateful for information which comes our way.

What then was going on already which contributed, or could contribute, towards the implementation of citizenship? The following might give a flavour:

■ Tutors, in the interest of continuity and progression, remain with the same tutor group (unless promotion or something similar intervenes!) throughout Years 7–11. This gives tutors a wonderful opportunity to get to know their tutees well throughout the course of their school careers. The tutees also get to know their tutors well. This relationship is crucially important as the pupils progress through the school and many of the demands of citizenship can be addressed through this relationship within the pastoral system.

■ There was an existing delivery of PSHE material by tutors to their tutor groups. This already delivered many of the requirements of citizenship. It is devised by year teams who arrange a handover of materials at the end of each year at a training day built into the school calendar. In this way the material delivered by one year's tutors is handed on to the next year's tutors at the end of the academic year. In this way time is made available for discussion and development of work.

■ There were a number of events already established and built in to the school calendar (including a number of those described within these two books). Care is taken to ensure that they do not conflict and the workload is spread.

■ We have created a strong feeling of pupil power in its best sense, ie a recognition by pupils that their opinions and suggestions are sought and valued. Pupils will not always get their own way, but if suggestions or requests cannot be accommodated (for whatever reason) a full and logical explanation is given. The work of the year and school councils, and the suggestions from tutor groups or individual pupils are taken seriously if they are forwarded through the appropriate channels. A number of examples are included in this book encompassing such areas as lunchtime arrangements, seating/social areas and the Buddy system.

- There is a 'can do' philosophy within the school body. Possibly this arises out of the sense of pupil power, but it appears in different guises. It has been seen in the work of some Year 10 pupils which resulted in changes to the school uniform, in the brainchild and hard work of one student that results in a whole new support system being established, in the sheer hard work of a group who put on the fashion show and in the voice of one Year 7 pupil who wished to look at the standard of food provided in the school canteen. This positive attitude is already in evidence in many areas and bodes well for the citizens of tomorrow.

- A thriving publication, *The Ammonite*, which goes out each week to pupils and parents and is a useful aid to communication. It informs pupils, students and parents about what is going on within the school community. It celebrates successes. It has published individual pieces of work. It has provided solace and support in times of sadness. It relates to our school and the wider community. It is citizenship in action.

- We have the Wellsway Community Development Group which is spearheading a Lottery Bid in order to provide a sports centre for the community. This is bringing together parents, pupils, teachers, governors and local businesses in an effort to improve facilities for a wide cross-section of people.

Many schools have these or similar things in operation. We must use them to help our introduction of citizenship. We felt that we had something to offer and these books are the result.

With apologies to Terry Waite, CBE quoted on page 13 of *Citizenship, The National Curriculum for England*, http://www.nc.uk.net, who said 'It is only when you know how to be a citizen of your own country that you can learn how to be a citizen of the world', we believe that being a citizen of your own school is invaluable in learning to become a citizen of your own country.

USING THIS BOOK

We believe that the material suggested in this book and the second book, *Activities for Teaching Citizenship in Secondary Schools*, which is more directly subject-related, provides activities and approaches that can be used very flexibly to cover subject specific, key skills and citizenship learning. The activities set out in this volume are focused towards the main issues of citizenship since they are whole-school activities (but will also undoubtedly be applicable in the transfer of key skills) while those in the second book will enable work in all three areas for learning. Part 4 of this book also gives some examples of possible class-based activities.

Part 1 provides background to the introduction of citizenship: Chapter 1 explains the requirements of citizenship and Chapter 2 is a look at the management issues surrounding its introduction. Chapters in Part 2 look at democracy in school and year councils and the election of school officers. Part 3 puts forward ideas for different activities within the school or at a large group level that can be used to assist the achievement of citizenship and, indeed, many other learning outcomes.

Use of activities

The most important thing to do to ensure the successful introduction of citizenship within a school is to take stock. The school will need to see what is already in existence and can be developed, made more explicit, relevant, enhanced or used in another way rather than to build a whole new set of activities and materials. Any gaps or deficiencies can then be identified and set in place to meet the requirements of citizenship at Key Stages 3 and 4. It is important that, as with any development, there is a sense of ownership. This does not mean that every school has to start from scratch. Co-operation and learning from each other is important in the classroom and also at a management level. This book and the activities described should provide a starting point for that learning. Within this context, the best people to know what needs to be done are the staff themselves, working within departments, faculties and year teams.

Schools have different strengths and priorities, each serves a different area with different cultural backgrounds and so the activities described will not always be of direct relevance. Therefore, the activities in this book, and its companion volume, are ones that give ideas and pointers as well as providing specific material. They are not intended to be prescriptive. They may be lifted directly from the page and put into practice in the school or in the classroom or used as templates for a wide range of similar activities which individual schools and teachers can create to meet their own teaching and learning goals more closely. If, as we hope, the book and its material appeal to teachers it will be useful both as a dip-in resource and as a prompt, or thought starter, for more different activities and lessons.

Differentiation

Within all of the activities we believe that there are indications of differentiation. In the whole-school activities, for example, the amount and type of the work undertaken by pupils can be directed. This is differentiation in action. For many of the whole-school activities, Key Stage 3 pupils work alongside Key Stage 4 pupils or even older pupils (see the Buddy system in Chapter 10, the Green Team in Chapter 9, the school council in Chapter 3, and the fashion show in Chapter 6) and differentiation can be introduced here by choosing tasks and inputs appropriate for individual pupils. As far as subject-specific opportunities are concerned, teachers will know the demands of the pupils and their abilities. The key issue is to adapt the work to match the needs of the pupils.

PART 1

BACKGROUND INFORMATION

CHAPTER 1

WHAT IS CITIZENSHIP?

This chapter sets out the citizenship requirements upon which the rest of the book is based. It is, therefore, written in a rather different style from the rest of the book which is intended to be a practical, dip-in resource for teachers. This chapter, by contrast, is necessarily based closely on the concise definition of citizenship used by the DfEE in the National Curriculum. We make no apology for this; it is essential to understand the requirement before trying to teach pupils something about their roles and duties as citizens. The full document can be obtained from the National Curriculum website on www.nc.uk.net.

Background

The report of the Advisory Group on Education for Citizenship and the Teaching of Democracy was delivered in September 1998. It recommended that the teaching of citizenship and democracy become a statutory requirement on schools. It identified three principal dimensions:

- participation in democracy;
- the responsibilities and rights of a citizen;
- the value of community activity.

The acceptance of this report by government has led to the development of a detailed citizenship curriculum for schools. This becomes mandatory in August 2002.

Citizenship and the National Curriculum

In their foreword to *Citizenship: The National Curriculum for England*, published in 1999, the Right Honourable David Blunkett, Secretary of State for Education and Employment and Sir William Stubbs, Chairman of the Qualifications and Curriculum Authority, refer to the equality of opportunity which underpins the school curriculum and of a commitment to valuing ourselves, our families and other relationships, the wider groups to which we belong, the diversity in our society and the environment in which we live.

The National Curriculum determines what should be taught in our schools and sets attainment targets for learning so that everyone has a shared understanding of the skills and knowledge that pupils should gain from their time in school. From September 2002 the curriculum will include citizenship. The aim is to provide pupils with an understanding of their roles and responsibilities as citizens in a modern democracy and so help them to deal with difficult moral and social questions that arise in their lives and in society.

Citizenship teaching, along with personal, social and health education (PSHE), is intended to give pupils the knowledge, skills and understanding to play an effective role in society at local, national and international levels. It should promote their spiritual, moral, social and cultural development and help them to live confident, healthy, independent lives, as individuals, parents, workers and members of society.

The programmes of study set out what pupils should be taught and the attainment targets set out the expected standards of pupils' performance. Programmes of study for Key Stages 3 and 4 are reproduced below.

In both cases citizenship teaching should ensure that knowledge and understanding about becoming informed citizens are acquired and applied when developing skills of enquiry and communication, and participation and responsible action.

PROGRAMME OF STUDY FOR CITIZENSHIP AT KEY STAGE 3

KNOWLEDGE AND UNDERSTANDING ABOUT BECOMING INFORMED CITIZENS

Pupils should be taught about:

- the legal and human rights and responsibilities underpinning society, basic aspects of the criminal justice system, and how both relate to young people;

- the diversity of national, regional, religious and ethnic identities in the United Kingdom and the need for mutual respect and understanding;

- central and local government, the public services they offer and how they are financed, and the opportunities to contribute;

- the key characteristics of parliamentary and other forms of government;

- the electoral system and the importance of voting;

- the work of community-based, national and international voluntary groups;

- the importance of resolving conflict fairly;

- the significance of the media in society;

- the world as a global community, and the political, economic, environmental and social implications of this, and the role of the European Union, the Commonwealth and the United Nations.

continued overleaf

continued

DEVELOPING SKILLS OF ENQUIRY AND COMMUNICATION

Pupils should be taught to:

- think about topical political, spiritual, moral, social and cultural issues, problems and events by analysing information and its sources, including ICT-based sources;

- justify orally and in writing a personal opinion about such issues, problems or events;

- contribute to group and exploratory class discussions, and take part in debates.

DEVELOPING SKILLS OF PARTICIPATION AND RESPONSIBLE ACTION

Pupils should be taught to:

- use their imagination to consider other people's experiences and be able to think about, express and explain views that are not their own;

- negotiate, decide and take part responsibly in both school and community-based activities;

- reflect on the process of participating.

PROGRAMME OF STUDY FOR CITIZENSHIP AT KEY STAGE 4

KNOWLEDGE AND UNDERSTANDING ABOUT BECOMING INFORMED CITIZENS

Pupils should be taught about:

- the legal and human rights and responsibilities underpinning society and how they relate to citizens, including the role and operation of the criminal and civil justice systems;

- the origins and implications of the diverse national, regional, religious and ethnic identities in the United Kingdom and the need for mutual respect and understanding;

- the work of parliament, the government and the courts in making and shaping the law;

- the importance of playing an active part in democratic and electoral processes;

- how the economy functions, including the role of business and financial services;

- the opportunities for individuals and voluntary groups to bring about social change locally, nationally, in Europe and internationally;

- the importance of a free press, and the media's role in society, including the Internet, in providing information and affecting opinion;

- the rights and responsibilities of consumers, employers and employees;

continued overleaf

continued

- the United Kingdom's relations in Europe, including the European Union, and relations with the Commonwealth and the United Nations;

- the wider issues and challenges of global interdependence and responsibility, including sustainable development and Local Agenda 21.

DEVELOPING SKILLS OF ENQUIRY AND COMMUNICATION

Pupils should be taught to:

- research a topical political, spiritual, moral, social or cultural issue, problem or event by analysing information from different sources, including ICT-based sources, showing an awareness of the use and abuse of statistics;

- express, justify and defend orally and in writing a personal opinion about such issues, problems or events;

- contribute to group and exploratory class discussions, and take part in formal debates.

DEVELOPING SKILLS OF PARTICIPATION AND RESPONSIBLE ACTION

Pupils should be taught to:

- use their imagination to consider other people's experiences and be able to think about, express, explain and critically evaluate views that are not their own;

- negotiate, decide and take part responsibly in school- and community-based activities;

- reflect on the process of participating.

Table 1.1. Summary of programmes of study for citizenship at Key Stages 3 and 4

Knowledge and understanding

Key Stage 3	Key Stage 4
Legal and human rights and responsibilities	Legal and human rights and responsibilities
Basic aspects of the criminal justice system	Operation of the criminal and civil justice systems
The diversity of national, regional, religious and ethnic identities in the UK	The origins and implications of the diverse national, regional, religious and ethnic identities in the UK
Central and local government public services	
Parliamentary and other forms of government	The work of parliament, the government and the courts in making law
The electoral system and voting	The electoral system and democratic process
Voluntary groups (community, national and international)	How individuals and voluntary groups can influence society
Conflict resolution	
Media in society	Media in society and the Internet
The world as a global community (EU, UN, Commonwealth)	Global interdependence and sustainable development (Local Agenda 21)
	The UK's relations in Europe and with the Commonwealth and UN
	How the economy functions, the role of business and financial services
	The rights and responsibilities of consumers, employers and employees

continued overleaf

Table 1.1. continued

Skills of enquiry and communication

Key Stage 3	**Key Stage 4**
Think and analyse information about topical issues, problems and events	Research and analyse information about topical issues, problems and events
Analyse information from ICT-based sources	Analyse information from different sources including ICT-based sources
Justify a personal opinion orally and in writing	Express, defend and justify a personal opinion orally and in writing
Contribute to group and class discussion	Contribute to group and class discussion
Take part in debates	Take part in formal debates

Skills of participation and responsible action

Key Stage 3	**Key Stage 4**
Use imagination to consider other people's experiences	Use imagination to consider other people's experiences
Think about, express and explain views that are not their own	Think about, express and explain and critically evaluate views that are not their own
Negotiate, decide and take part responsibly in school- and community-based activities	Negotiate, decide and take part responsibly in school- and community-based activities
Reflect on the process of participation	Reflect on the process of participation

Attainment targets

The types and range of performance that pupils should be able to demonstrate at the end of the key stages are broadly similar.

For Key Stage 3 they are as follows:

- Pupils have a broad knowledge and understanding of the topical events they study:

    - *the rights, responsibilities and duties of citizens;*

    - *the role of the voluntary sector;*

    - *forms of government;*

    - *provision of public services and the criminal and legal systems.*

- They show how the public gets information and how opinion is formed and expressed, including through the media.

- They show understanding of how and why changes take place in society.

- Pupils take part in school and community-based activities, demonstrating personal and group responsibility in their attitudes to themselves and others.

Key Stage 4 differs only in the depth of understanding required.

- A 'comprehensive' knowledge and understanding is required.

- In addition, pupils are required to obtain and use information from different sources.

- They also need to reflect on and critically evaluate what they learn and what they do.

CHAPTER 2

MANAGEMENT ISSUES

Teaching citizenship should not, we believe, become a mountain for schools to climb. However, realistically, there will need to be some changes to the way things are done.

The key areas for consideration include:

- introducing/consolidating citizenship into the curriculum;

- the links to key skills;

- resources;

- staff development;

- stakeholders.

These we will examine in turn.

Introducing and consolidating citizenship into the curriculum

There will need to be a well-managed process to introduce or consolidate the teaching of citizenship in the school if it is to become an effective and all-inclusive part of the school's activities. Like any change, the introduction of these new ideas will need to be managed. The management of change can be difficult and there can be pain.

There are several implementation issues that should be considered when trying to introduce citizenship in a systematic way or to consolidate what is already being done. These are likely to be:

■ managing yet another initiative or 'initiative fatigue';

■ the cross-curricular challenge;

■ the incorporation of existing good practice within the school.

Managing another initiative

Most schools will have agreed aims for the conduct of their activities. These will have been arrived at in a variety of different ways, but most schools will have agreed their aims through discussion and negotiation amongst pupils/ students/ staff/parents/governors. By the very nature of the constitution of the governing body, that discussion will have brought in the views of the wider community. Where there has been such involvement from a wide cross-section of people, there will be a commitment to achieving these aims from a whole community who will all be working towards the same end. Therefore, citizenship is likely already to have been accepted as an integral part of what the school is trying to achieve. This will manifest itself in some or all of the following or similar aims:

■ to enable all young people to achieve their full potential academically, emotionally, physically and spiritually;

■ to foster the development of personal moral values;

■ to develop a sense of self-esteem and the habits of self-discipline;

■ to promote creative and aesthetic awareness and enjoyment;

■ to develop a wide range of skills in communication;

■ to develop respect for other people and the environment and an awareness of rights and responsibilities;

■ to encourage active citizenship – participation in decision-making and the democratic process;

- to educate young people to respect and value other cultures and to be aware of issues relating to the wider community;

- to foster positive links with the local community;

- to educate for and practise equality of opportunity;

- to prepare young people effectively for the demands of a rapidly changing high-technology society;

- to promote a healthy lifestyle;

- to encourage independent lifelong learning.

The introduction of the teaching of citizenship can be directly compared and aligned with the teaching of key skills and can be seen as another, cross-curricular, layer or learning stream to complement and enhance what is already being done in the classroom. Rather than being seen as a whole new subject area it should be viewed as a way of approaching a more holistic view of education and a route towards more 'joined up' teaching.

It will be important, in order to gain commitment and ownership, to involve staff in the process and encourage them to develop material within their own subject specialism which will facilitate the drawing out of subject-specific, key skills and citizenship lessons. Planning time should be made available for these activities. Availability of such time will be limited but it is suggested that INSET time be set aside for departments to develop their own approaches and materials. We hope that this book and its sister volume will seed and inform that thinking while providing a versatile bank of material and ideas for use.

The cross-curricular challenge

With increasing emphasis being placed on results, and the measurement of results being a key performance indicator, it is inevitable that departments will wish to concentrate on delivery of the National Curriculum since results in that area will be the primary measure of their performance. However, there are distinct pressures from government, and therefore from OFSTED, to deliver rounded education in a more 'joined-up' fashion. The key skills approach is an example, citizenship is another.

Figure 2.1 shows the relationships between various activities in schools and it is clear that the obstacles to effective cross-curricular working will appear between departments.

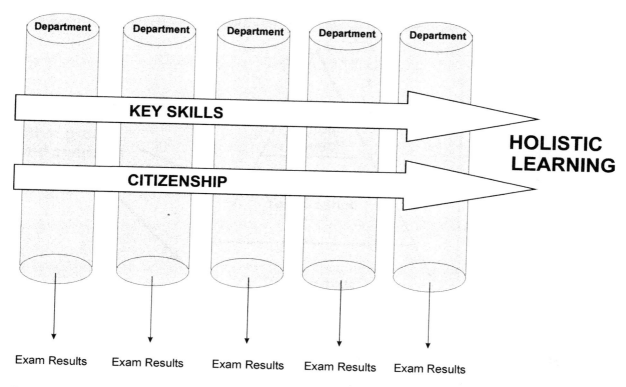

Figure 2.1 The relationship between various school activities

Therefore, the impact of citizenship as an extra burden must be reduced and we believe that this is best done through the use of activities and materials that will encourage concurrent learning in all three fields:

■ subject;

■ key skills;

■ citizenship.

The incorporation of existing good practice within the school

It is very likely that every school will already be doing things, as part of PSHE lessons or elsewhere, that will contribute to the needs of citizenship teaching and it would be a great shame if these were to be abandoned in some flurry of enthusiastic new activity. It is essential for departments to audit or take stock of their materials and methods to see just how much or how little new material needs to be incorporated. Minimizing the extra workload must be a priority. The audit approach will help to do that and it should also give recognition to those who have developed good material that can be copied and shared. A small group of champions, led perhaps by the PSHE department if there is one, could control such an audit and ensure that existing good practice is recognized, shared and that the effort of origination and development of activities is not duplicated in different departments. Often ideas in one subject area are easily translated into another without the need for prolonged creative thought. INSET time can also be used for this process of sharing good practice.

The links to key skills

The key skills area is one that already has a high profile at Key Stage 5. Key Stage 5 key skills qualification is worth up to 60 UCAS points. In order for students to reach this high level, it is vital that they develop both the key skills and a cross-curricular approach to learning at Key Stages 3 and 4. The post-16 changes, implemented in September 2000, emphasize the importance of communication, working with others, application of number, information technology, problem-solving and improving one's own learning alongside A levels and other courses. These areas form an integral part of the curriculum and have obvious links with citizenship at Key Stages 3 and 4. As such, key skills and citizenship can be seen as mutually supportive, each feeding the other. There is, or can be, a symbiotic relationship between citizenship and key skills. Some schools are already recognizing and/or accrediting key skills both at Key Stage 4 and Key Stage 5. Methods of doing this vary. Key skills can, for example, be recognized and identified at the end of a particular course or piece of work, or there may be an input to give pupils the opportunity to demonstrate key skills – a project for example, which could be teacher guided or supported self-study. Citizenship could be used here. It could be a vehicle for demonstrating key skills or key skills could be used as research aids. Taking this model a stage further, if key skills are recognized or accredited then so too could citizenship. To minimize the workload, an area or areas of citizenship and an area of key skills could be negotiated with each department. They then develop an activity to cover both and fulfil the requirements to gain key-skills accreditation.

Resources

Co-ordination of the approach

It would be very easy for each department/area in a school to carry out an audit and simply tick boxes. For example, if a history department, at Key Stage 3, looks at the development of universal suffrage, it can claim it has 'done' democracy. As all Key Stage 3 teachers teach this element then all teachers too have 'done' democracy and so have all Key Stage 3 pupils. *Wrong!* There is an issue of coordination within the department to ensure the information is put in the context of the twenty-first century to show its importance to today's citizens, perhaps in the light of rights and responsibilities. This can be achieved quite easily by formal or informal discussion at department meetings or elsewhere. Time must be set aside for departments to address the contribution they can, or could, make to citizenship. For most departments we suggest there should be 'obvious' areas and guidelines available to help in this. However, a whole-school approach should help identify and plan the time available and give clear guidelines for departments to use (see 'Staff development' below).

Co-ordination across departments

It is always useful to know what other departments are doing so that good practice can be shared. To re-teach something which has been covered elsewhere is a waste of valuable time. Using what has been taught elsewhere can be built upon to help pupils make connections and break down barriers between subjects or 'de-compartmentalize' them. For citizenship this is even more important. Coordination across departments is difficult and could be very time consuming so a simple list of the topics addressed in each year or across a key stage by each subject area could be published. A year planner in a year office or in the staff-room could be utilized to display the topics under discussion in each area. Teachers straying into areas of possible overlap are, therefore, forewarned and can discuss with their colleagues what has been covered and in which way.

Overview

Unlike departmental schemes of work, which are regularly reviewed at departmental meetings (through common assessment and testing and through shared discussions), it is much less easy to have an overview of a cross-curricular topic. It may be appropriate for either the key skills and/or PSHE coordinators within a school to take responsibility for the overview of citizenship teaching as there are so many obvious links with these subjects. Another possibility is for an existing team or working party to extend its brief. Citizenship could fit easily within a guidance review team or a careers guidance orbit, or it might become a significant part of the responsibilities of pastoral heads of Key Stage 3 and Key Stage 4. The important point is that there will need to be a whole-school overview of citizenship activity within the school and existing structures should be used wherever possible, rather than new or specifically created working parties or groups, to carry out this function.

Ensuring universal coverage

At Key Stage 3, all pupils will have access to citizenship teaching through PSHE and within subject areas. Thus it is safe to assume that, providing the aspects of co-ordination and overview discussed above have been addressed, all pupils will have been taught citizenship. At Key Stage 4, however, because not all pupils follow the same curriculum, this is not the case. All pupils do, however, study English, maths, science, a modern foreign language, a technology subject and religious education. Most schools have a PSHE programme in place and this can be modified to address significant areas. To ensure that all Key Stage 4 pupils will have access to citizenship teaching there will be a greater onus on teachers in those subject areas to consider citizenship in their lessons. This issue will need to be addressed by the school and Key Stage 4 co-ordinators to ensure equality of access.

Staff development

Awareness and recognition of achievements to date

This is a very important first step in the process of the introduction or consolidation of citizenship teaching and of the audit which is so important to answer the question 'Where are we now?' Many departments will already have begun to look at their involvement in citizenship. Perhaps there has already been work done in this area under a different guise – equal opportunities, for example, or some aspect of the legacy of TVEI (Technical and Vocational Education Initiative) in which schools were encouraged to look at political awareness, at work-related activities and at education for industrial understanding. The legacy from some of these initiatives, with subsequent development, could quite easily feed into citizenship. Time spent reflecting on what has already been achieved is time well spent. This reflection will de-mystify and improve the general understanding of what citizenship really means. It will recognize the work done and raise the profile of relevant activities and in so doing will reassure staff that citizenship is not necessarily some huge mountain to climb; teams will probably discover that they are already well on the way up the slope.

Attitudes/departmental myopia

It is understandable that the priority of every department will be teaching their specific subject. Standard attainment tests at Key Stage 3 and GCSE results, not to mention league tables, dictate this. It is well known that departments never have enough time, but some must be made available to ensure that the necessary audits and re-direction of resources can and do occur. A whole-school approach is the best way of making sure this time is made available. Thus all departments, at their next departmental meeting, could be required to have a specific 'citizenship' agenda or time could be made available for departments to discuss specific citizenship issues on a training day.

Once time has been made available, the first barrier for all to overcome is the mind-set that suggests citizenship is an additional burden to a teacher or that it is an area which 'other departments' can/should address (the inference being 'but not us'). Some subject areas, like business studies and history, for example, might more naturally assimilate the citizenship agenda than others. However, all areas can contribute, utilizing their existing schemes of work. Within a school, it would be very helpful if a specific individual (eg the PSHE co-ordinator, Key Stage 3 co-ordinator, key skills co-ordinator), who has attended courses relating to citizenship and is part of the co-ordinating team or structure within the school, is able to make an input into different departments if difficulties are perceived.

Use of INSET days

The culture of the school will best indicate the format of a training day. It may be appropriate to invite input from an external 'expert' or, alternatively, to provide home-grown material. Either approach, or indeed a mix of the two, has merit but in any event this really is a situation in which the much talked about 'sense of ownership' is vitally important.

Suggestions for inclusion in such a training day could be:

- Compilation of achievements to date within the context of citizenship and recognition of them. This would help to develop a checklist of useful activities. An example is shown below. This could be achieved by:

    - *discussion by a team of a pre-prepared list, perhaps the staff development team, curriculum team, PSHE team, etc;*

    - *brainstorming to create a list on the day using information from all colleagues. This could then be put into a semblance of order and distributed following the training day;*

    - *convening small groups, either subject based or cross-curricular, to work together to assemble ideas and then share them in a plenary session.*

- Input from 'an expert' or someone within the school showing how citizenship can be an integral part of a lesson. Within any school there will be departments which are already more in tune/comfortable with the ideas and concepts of citizenship. Arranging for someone who has already adopted good practice in the teaching of citizenship to present their ideas to the rest of their colleagues is a superb professional development opportunity and a chance for departments to share their expertise with others. Depending upon the people involved, strategies might include:

    - *use of an overhead projector, a lesson plan talked through;*

> – sharing of resources, looking at how one particular aspect of the lesson has been addressed;
>
> – identifying pupils' work where citizenship has clearly made an impact.

- A variation on the above might be to use the same approach but have colleagues from more than one department who have collaborated/are collaborating on a particular issue present the lessons from their experience.

- An input from the key skills co-ordinator, or another member of staff with a specific interest in this area, to talk through and demonstrate the links between key skills and citizenship. One way of doing this might be to show, for example, how using ICT skills can produce a series of graphs, spreadsheets, charts and so on to support work on local government and elections. If the finished product was to be presented to a class by the pupil(s) involved, then more key-skills targets are met alongside the greater understanding of this aspect of citizenship.

- Time made available for departments to think about how they would address a particular topic within the citizenship remit. If this was a time-limited exercise there could be the opportunity for two or three groups to give a brief presentation on their work.

- Alternatively, make time available for the same purpose to cross-curricular groups.

The example on the opposite page is by no means exhaustive but it gives a flavour of the many and diverse activities that already occur in most schools and which already make a contribution to the teaching of citizenship. Most of these topics are covered in later chapters of this book.

Stakeholders

There are two significant stakeholder groups:

- governors;
- parents.

EXAMPLE

An example of a possible checklist of activities identified or generated to help the systematic introduction or consolidation of the teaching of citizenship within the school:

THE SUBJECT AUDIT	the first step to answering 'Where are we now?'
PSHE AUDIT	a way of addressing any areas not covered in specific subjects
KEY SKILLS AUDIT	each school probably already has a method of accrediting/assessing key skills
CAREERS CALENDAR CHECKLIST ESPECIALLY AT KEY STAGE 4	Most schools already deliver work experience placements (one or two weeks) and may also offer opportunities for work shadowing and interview experience
'SPECIALIST' DAYS OR CONFERENCES	these can take a variety of formats and can be at Key Stage 3 or Key Stage 4. Areas which could be addressed are industry day, religious education/philosophy and belief conference, environmental awareness day, mock elections
EXTRACURRICULAR ACTIVITIES	plays with a specific message, debating societies and debating forum, charity collections and support for charities, field trips, Duke of Edinburgh Award
SPECIFIC ACTIVITIES	school and/or year council, Young Enterprise, 'Buddy' system, foreign exchanges/visits
WORKING WITH OUTSIDE AGENCIES	bank set up within the school, support for charities, assemblies used as a platform for

continued

continued

	organizations, eg Relate, AL Anon and Alateen, Childline, Cruse, etc.
OTHERS	study days, activities week, presentation evenings

CITIZENSHIP AUDIT

Which ever way the audit is approached, or whichever strategies are employed, the end result should be threefold:

■ all teachers are more comfortable with issues within the citizenship umbrella;

■ departments start or continue sharing information;

■ all teachers are aware of the wide variety of whole-school activities addressing citizenship issues that are going on in their school so that appropriate links can be made.

The role of each is described below.

Governors

The introduction/amplification of citizenship in the curriculum for Key Stage 3 and Key Stage 4 will clearly have implications for the governing body. The governors' curriculum committee or its equivalent will need to be kept aware of developments and also be kept informed of the method of delivery. It may be that a particular governor would want to be, or could be encouraged to be, the 'link' governor.

The governing body, however, could play a more active and involved role in citizenship. Many schools are fortunate enough to have governors who are currently in or recently retired from industry, local government, legal or other relevant professions. Consequently, they have much knowledge, many skills and useful contacts. They may also have time available. As governors, they have already shown commitment to the school and some may well wish to express this commitment further and use their expertise to support citizenship teaching.

We suggest a number of ways in which this expertise can be used:

- *Involvement in mock interviews for Key Stage 4 pupils.* Depending upon the time available these can include a number of elements. The mock interview could mirror exactly a real situation with a job advert, letter of application, interview and a realistic debrief. If time does not permit, it could be a less-demanding exercise with a more general situation discussing interview techniques. The more realistic the situation can be made, however, the more effective it will be.

- *Use of contacts to create situations which give pupils a deeper understanding of the wider community.* These can be many and varied. For Key Stage 4 pupils, for example, groups could be involved in a design project with a local firm, work shadowing could be set up with a variety of occupations or a group could visit a local charity or care establishment. The problem with creating situations like these is that they are often, for practical reasons, limited to small numbers. Situations can be set up within the classroom with the advantage of reaching greater numbers, but realism may be lost.

- *Explore the idea of governors as link tutors for a year group or tutor group.* This would not only bring them into more direct personal contact with pupils, but would also help provide the wider context and perspective from legal, social, business and economic institutions. With this link established, more opportunities for interchange can be identified. Some suggestions for further development of this role of link tutor could be:

    - *Involvement in the PSHE programmes, particularly focusing on those elements relating to citizenship. In this way the link governor becomes a source of information and a facilitator.*

– Working with members of the tutor group to produce an assembly with a citizenship theme to be put on before the whole year group.

– Working with the tutor group to help raise money for a local/national/international charity. Matched funding arrangements could be negotiated here. If, for example, a school works with a local business or industry to raise funds for a local charity, then there is a pleasing result in that two distinct strands, education and business, come together to help a third in the wider community.

– Use of governors in appropriate lessons to encourage pupils to look at the wider perspective. This may develop into a series of lessons relating to the particular topic.

■ Liaison between a named governor and a specific department/area within the school. Attendance of that governor at department meetings when specific topics/issues are being discussed could bring about a 'citizenship' slant. Similarly, if whole or part of a training day was being used for department time on a particular topic, governors' involvement could contribute much.

Parents

Parents too have a huge contribution they can make in this area. The Home School Agreement, negotiated between parents, pupils and school, is in itself a classic example of citizenship in action, recognizing as it does rights and responsibilities in all three parties forming the partnership.

In many ways, parents can be involved in citizenship activities in much the same way as governors. There is, however, one additional area of input parents may be able to make. This is in providing an insight into different cultural, religious and ethnic backgrounds. The calendar provides many opportunities for this, eg Chinese New Year (possibly through philosophy and belief, drama or art), Thanksgiving Day (possibly through history/English), Saints' Days, Bastille Day (through modern languages), Passover and Diwali, etc. In practice, this could range from bringing in costumes, artefacts and pictures to cooking a meal or re-enacting a situation.

PART 2

DEMOCRACY IN SCHOOLS

CHAPTER 3

ESTABLISHING EFFECTIVE YEAR AND SCHOOL COUNCILS

This chapter sets out the issues surrounding the establishment of a school council and associated year councils and the mechanisms through which this can be achieved. The formal extraction of the citizenship learning that the working of the school council will prompt should be simple and can be done using reflection at tutor and year group meetings.

Issues

Purpose and policy

A school needs to be very clear about the purpose of a school council and year councils, and the way that they are to be established will need to support the aims of the school. There are a variety of possible aims and it should be possible to incorporate them all if required. Some of the most common are:

- to discuss and review matters relating to pupil welfare in discussion with the pupils themselves;

- to identify and discuss concerns raised by pupils;

- to give responses to whole-school issues to the school management team as a way of polling opinion across the whole school.

At the time the council is established its aims and purpose should be made clear to all. It may be appropriate to develop a constitution as part of the initial meetings of the council.

Structure and composition

A tried-and-tested model provides a three-tier, progressive system of representation and discussion, as shown in Figure 3.1.

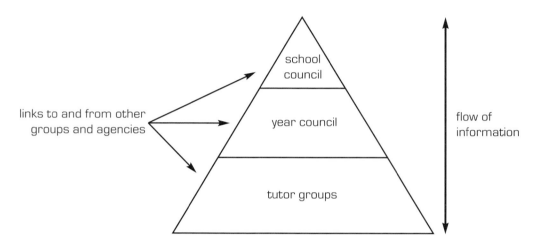

Figure 3.1 The three-tier flow of information

Tutor groups form the basic units where issues can be raised and discussions and decisions made in 'higher' forums are communicated. Each tutor group in Years 7–11 selects two representatives (ideally one male and one female) to attend the regular year-council meetings. These are pre-planned events and they should take place before school council meetings. Each year-council elects two representatives to take forward their year's views to the school council whose meetings are also pre-planned at a frequency that is felt to be appropriate. With this organization of the school council, all pupils have access to it through the year council. Communication is two-way and can also be widely disseminated through other meetings and groups as appropriate. Issues can be identified at all levels, tutor group, year council and school council. The meeting of tutor groups will inform year councils which in turn feed the school council. The school council will debate issues brought forward and the results will be passed back through year-council meetings for representatives to report back to tutor groups. This process ensures integration across all years and groups so that they become 'part of what goes on here'

Election or selection

If the year council is to be taken seriously, the tutor group representatives, in the first instance, do need to be elected according to a formal process. The year-representatives who go forward to the school council (and in this model it is ideally two, one male and one female) can be decided by various means. Each year- council has autonomy to decide this and methods vary from election, self-selection, suggestion or rotation. The selection process itself can, obviously, provide many lessons about democratic processes.

In order for the process to be inclusive, tutors at all levels must exercise vigilance in the election process initially. Guidance will be required, as will encouragement of less-confident pupils. The methods that might possibly be used to identify the two year representatives for the school council include:

■ *Election:* a vote is taken among the representatives on the year council. Each has two votes to cast in a secret ballot to decide who are the two most suitable candidates to go to the school council based upon their view of the people who have made the greatest contribution to the year council. However, as in all elections, each elector may have a very individual reason for making his or her choice. Guidelines should perhaps indicate that there should be one female and one male representative to go forward to the school council.

In the event of a tie, the member of staff in charge of the council may have the casting vote. Alternatively, some form of transferable vote could be incorporated in the case of a tie.

■ *Selection:* pupils who have already been very closely identified with a major issue might usefully be selected on the basis that someone who feels strongly about an issue may be the best advocate for it.

■ *Suggestion:* particular council representatives may be chosen on the grounds that they have a high school profile in another area and so it is felt that they have the necessary 'street cred'. For example, an individual might be well known because of sporting prowess, being a member of the debating team, having strong musical ability or being seen in drama productions.

- *Rotation:* there may well be some very positive reasons why rotation is chosen as a method of identifying the year-representatives who will go to the school council. There is the issue of sharing expertise and giving more people the chance to be involved in democratic debate within a school setting. However, experience has shown that rotation has sometimes been used because pupils do not wish to make a long-term commitment. The drawbacks are the lack of continuity and a potential loss of time taken up by the need to go over old ground.

In both year and school councils the role of the chairperson becomes very important. Each school is different and there will be different rationales behind the appointment of appropriate chairpersons. It may be that it should be a head of year or a year tutor. It could start off with one of these and then the role of Chairperson switch to a pupil or it might be a pupil from the beginning. Whichever model is to be used there have to be guidelines concerning the rules of debate and ensuring fairness.

Credibility

In order to have any credibility a school council must achieve, and be seen to achieve, change. If it does not, pupils will have little or no faith in it. It must also, however, work within the context of the school and its normal constraints, rules, regulations and practices that cannot be ignored. It will, therefore, have to face the problem of potentially conflicting demands. It must also recognize that its work will outlast that particular council population and affect many, possibly generations of pupils to come. Thus it has a responsibility to these pupils as well as to the current year groups. This involves an injection of realism and some of the ways in which this can be achieved have been addressed below.

It is crucial that a school council is an integral part of the culture, ethos and organization of the school. If it is a 'bolt on' initiative, it will not prove successful. The council needs to operate within the institution, supporting the aims and recognizing the importance of the pupil/parent/school partnership. For this reason there have to be clear and obvious links between the council and other groups and teams within the school. The council has to build upon ideas and suggestions, forwarding them if necessary and appropriate, or responding with reasoned arguments for not progressing issues. In order for the process to be fully inclusive, and for all pupils to contribute both to the election of representatives and to the debates, there will need to be a mechanism to push opinion up the chain to the council and down again to all the pupils.

How, then, does the council gain and retain credibility and relevance? Clearly if it is to have some real impact on events and be taken seriously, by staff as well as pupils, the school must consider how to embed the council and to ensure that its standing is enhanced. This can be done in a variety of ways:

- by ensuring that its achievements are relevant, significant, noticeable and celebrated;

- by election of members at tutor group level so that it has an impact on all pupils' lives;

- by being able to identify tasks which can be delegated to a member of staff to carry out;

- by being taken seriously by school staff who may be interviewed/sought out to impart information to school or year council representatives;

- by the use of identification badges (similar in appearance to school sports colours or school office-holder badges);

- by being able to bid for funding for a particular project, eg from the PTA;

- by being able to invite staff to attend meetings and give an input. (An invitation should never be turned down!);

- by ensuring that everything is reported back to the tutor groups;

- by use of a School Council Action Sheet if it is necessary to find out more information about a particular issue/question. This is used as the basis for a report back and so gives responsibility to representatives.

A copy of a School Council Action Sheet is shown overleaf in Figure 3.2. This has been designed to be simple. When a question is raised a member of the school council is chosen to carry out the task of following up the issue under discussion by making contact with a certain member of the school staff, arranging a meeting

SCHOOL COUNCIL ACTION SHEET

Council representative:

Person(s) to see:

Questions or subject of enquiry:

Findings or results of the enquiries:

Subsequent actions:

Figure 3.2 School council action sheet

at which they can ask pertinent questions, seek advice, request information, ask for an explanation or discover the rationale behind a school policy or rule.

It is then the responsibility of that individual to return to the school council with the answer. The people approached for answers will vary; it might be the head or deputy head, it could be any member of the teaching staff, the caretaking staff, a governor or members of the PTA. Those seeking the answers range from Year 7 to Year 11 pupils and the issues that they are tasked to address might encompass a wide range of possible areas including uniform, toilets, provision of school lunches, access to telephones and examination arrangements. The list is endless.

Communication

Clearly a key issue is the communication of the business of the school council to all. Without effective communication the council will quickly become irrelevant and sidelined. There are a variety of possible methods, more than one of which will almost certainly be needed. These include:

- year representatives reporting back to tutor groups;

- minutes produced by council members available within one week of the meeting and accessible to all;

- adding school council issues or decisions to the agendas of other appropriate meetings;

- passing messages and decisions from the school council in communications to pupils and staff at assemblies and staff briefings, bulletins and other means;

- making School Council Action Sheets available for all members of councils;

- regular briefing to parents on issues highlighted at school council meetings;

- recognition of the differences made by the council, eg physical differences observed such as the provision of seating;

- through the obvious support from members of staff.

Highlighting the learning

The council will, of course, have an intrinsic value of its own and make a real contribution to the life of the school if it is properly set up and managed and its discussions remain relevant and significant. However, there also needs to be some overt, explicit learning about citizenship to be extracted from the process. The similarities to political and democratic processes elsewhere may not be immediately apparent to all pupils. Staff involved in the process will need to highlight the issues of democracy, representation, constituencies and different needs and perspectives whenever they can. There are plenty of opportunities for this:

- when representatives report back to year and tutor groups;

- while establishing and maintaining the etiquette of debate used in the council meetings (and to some degree in 'lower' meetings);

- making some of the lessons explicit in school council minutes;

- explaining the use of the democratic system of elections in the school and the similarities to national and local democratic processes;

- encouraging all pupils to chair meetings or contribute formally in some way;

- rotation of pupils as minutes secretary;

- using information and evidence gathered from the wider world to support or refute a matter under discussion;

- creating sub-groups to address particular issues, eg the creation of a Year 11 group to organize the Year 11 leavers' ball or the creation of a sub-group to plan charity events.

Achievement of a solution focus rather than one of complaint

There will always be some concern that the school council could become a place of complaint. If it degenerates into a forum only to raise the complaints of the aggrieved it will become totally discredited. Care must be taken to re-inforce the role of the council, and other actions to support its more beneficial contribution could be:

- to remind pupils of the aims of the school and to reinforce the work of the council in this context by emphasizing the role for which it was created;

- to share information, to explain matters fully and put issues in context. Finance, for example, can be a constraint on good ideas, as can practicalities and logistics which have to be accepted as reality;

- to encourage representatives to talk to those with the expert knowledge and information who can help bring about a solution or compromise, eg superintendent of premises, health and safety co-ordinator, outside agency (for an example, see the case study on installing a payphone below);

- celebrating and publicizing successes;

- encouraging the pupils to take responsibility for their own research, eg School Council Action Sheet (see above);

- allowing real debate;

- using the example of previous years' experienced representatives as a role model.

Training for council participants

Clearly there must be training, help, support and advice for council members. This will be crucial in the early days but, since a regular change of members is to be encouraged to extend the numbers of pupils participating (although some people will need to be members for several sessions in order to become experienced role models), on-going training will be required. This will need to cover among other issues:

- involvement in the democratic process of elections;

- rotation of those chairing meetings;

- routine briefing on council rules and debating etiquette;

- discussions with tutor/learning co-ordinator/head of year/assistant head teacher/pupil support;

- attendance at and presentations to various committees.

It is suggested that this briefing, familiarization and training be carried out as part of and in preparation for selection of representatives to the year council and to the school council. This will take place, therefore, as part of tutor group sessions and requires that tutors are both familiar with the working of the council and supportive of its aims and procedures in order to promote it in a positive way.

Mechanisms

Involvement of management staff, teachers and school officers

Staff and school officers will be invited for specific meetings/agenda items. Ideally one member of staff should be present at all meetings (but see Home School Agreement page 41). It may be appropriate for a member of the senior management team to be the staff member attending the school council. The role of that staff member progresses from the chairperson, at the beginning of the year, to adviser or observer as the pupils accept and take more responsibility for the process. For some debates, however, it may be appropriate for the representatives to meet without the presence of a member of staff. This would not be easily possible in the early meetings in a year if the levels of experience were low.

Chairing meetings

Initially year council and school council meetings should be chaired by a member of staff. A year tutor, learning co-ordinator or head of year could be appointed as the chairperson for year councils. The assistant head teacher (pupil support) would probably chair the first school council meeting of the academic year. The second school council meeting would be chaired by a Year 11 pupil, the third by a Year 10 pupil and so on until all years have been represented. By the sixth school council meeting of the academic year it would be chaired by a Year 7 pupil. By this time he or she would have witnessed other pupils in the role of chairperson and become more confident within the council.

Decision-making

The rules for decision-making need to be clearly mapped out (in the constitution if there is to be one). Possible routes to obtaining a decision may be:

- *consensus* – realistically, that may be hard to achieve;

- *majority voting* – this is straightforward but may leave 49 per cent unhappy;

- *specifically agreed voting powers and vetoes* – the right of veto would ordinarily be held by staff but would have to be exercised only rarely and in the context of a very clear and straightforward explanation of the reasons for it.

Setting agendas and raising issues

Normally individuals or tutor groups will raise issues of concern and these are then taken to year council unless they can be resolved immediately. They are debated at this stage and a decision whether or not to forward the matter to the school council is made depending on the nature and impact of the issue. Occasionally, issues may be introduced by a member of staff, for example a health and safety problem, Home School Agreement or other similar topics which require an airing and general acceptance before adoption.

Rules and etiquette

To some extent these have already been alluded to. However, a pupil coming as a new year representative would need some guidelines on procedure. In some schools a formal constitution might be the answer. Other schools might like something a little less institutionalized; a constitution could be quite daunting, especially for younger pupils. The following guidelines for debate might be useful:

- Each tutor group representative needs to be made aware that his or her role is to listen to ideas and concerns within the tutor group in order to be able to represent those in some way to the year council. Here the work of tutors is important in making sure that the tutor group debate allows pupils to be heard and perhaps to make explicit the consensus or diversity of views. The tutor group representatives need to go to the year council armed with this information. (It is worth remembering that agenda items can be suggested by tutor groups and that issues to be discussed will usually be identified in advance.)

- At the year/school council meetings the rules of debate need to be made clear. The representative who tabled the concern should be listened to without interruptions. Other representatives are then asked to give their views. Sometimes this is by rotation (which has the advantage that everyone has a turn to speak) but it can also be by indication of response from other representatives who will signal their wish to speak. The chairperson should be on the look out, if this is the method chosen, to ensure that everyone has the opportunity to speak.

- Only one person should be speaking at any one time. This ensures that all views are heard and it encourages others to listen and argue against something rationally and sensibly rather than shout an argument down. The chairperson controls the session.

- Minutes are taken. This can be done by council representatives in rotation or by having a non-speaking additional pupil or adult in the room. These minutes describe the outline of the discussion and identify action points. Often these action points involve the use of the School Council Action Sheet (see above) and a timescale is set for reporting back.

The school council in the following case studies has also been involved in the provision of extra litterbins and seating for pupils, and the relocation and improved security of the bicycle sheds. The latter involved the use of a school council-inspired questionnaire to pupils and liaison with the community police officer. Examples of other issues, all originating with pupils, are an offensive against chewing gum and liaison with the school kitchen concerning the quality, variety and price of school meals.

CASE STUDY: HOME SCHOOL AGREEMENT

In this case the school council was the body through which pupils identified the pledges they would make for the Home School Agreement. In order to do this there was initial discussion within tutor groups. The tutor group representatives took the ideas generated to the year council, where they were debated, and then on to the school council. This particular meeting was chaired by a Year 11 pupil and there were no members of staff present. The agreed pledges were then forwarded to the school management team. No changes were made (except those of literary style in order to ensure consistency of presentation) and the pledges in their entirety were accepted as part of the Home School Agreement and subsequently printed in the pupils' homework diary.

CASE STUDY: CHANGE IN UNIFORM TO ALLOW GIRLS TO WEAR TROUSERS

This debate took place in the context of a governors' subcommittee having made a recent pronouncement on uniform guidelines which did not include trousers for girls. The issue was raised again at the Year 10 council who brought it to the school council. Having gained support here, a group of Year 10 council representatives prepared a presentation for the head teacher and were asked to put their views to the governors' personnel committee. The governors subsequently agreed that girls could wear trousers. The resultant newspaper publicity recognized this as an example of democracy in action through the school council.

Variation and innovation

There is a wide range of possible variations on this theme to meet the needs of different schools. These include:

- arrangements for sixth-form inclusion in an 11–18 school;

- in smaller schools more than two representatives from each tutor group may go to year councils (The size of the year council on which this model is based is 16, with two from each tutor group. The size of the school council is 12, two from each year group 7–11 and two sixth-form students.);

- it may be appropriate to combine year council meetings to represent Key Stage 3 and Key Stage 4 rather than separate years;

- a written constitution can be a great help but would require careful drafting. This might form a valuable project for a subcommittee;

- creating a relationship with the local paper so that there is a regular input reporting on the work of the councils (schools' page, for example);

- regular inputs from outside agencies and others (eg the local residents association, community police, or a representative from the PTA) in order to share information and views and get feedback from the community about the way the school is perceived;

- involvement of partner primary schools at occasional sessions;

- the provision of a defined budget over which the council has control as an addition to any discretionary funding that may be available to be bid for.

CASE STUDY: CONDITION OF SCHOOL TOILETS

Concerns about the condition of a particular block of toilets were raised by a tutor group and subsequently taken to the year and school councils. The response, after discussion, was to 'reclaim' the toilets and to keep them free from rubbish and acts of minor vandalism like graffiti and damage to drinking fountains. The superintendent of premises was asked to attend a school council meeting to give advice and make an input and he then reported back to the governors' premises committee. The school council took the view that money spent on renovating toilets was money taken directly from education and that this could not and should not be allowed. Tutor group representatives returned to tutor groups fired up with information and enthusiasm to encourage everyone to be engaged actively in taking on responsibility for the toilets and reporting any incident of ill use. It was arranged that time would be made available for tutor group representatives to talk to all tutor groups at the same time, with tutors actively involved to ensure fair hearing and comment. So far this campaign is working.

CASE STUDY: INSTALLATION OF A PAYPHONE FOR PUPILS' USE

The need for a payphone was identified, as mobile phones are banned in school as in most schools, and pupils contacted BT and researched the feasibility and cost of installing one. The preferred location was not possible because of additional wiring costs. A compromise was arrived at and the payphone is now fully operational.

SCHOOL COUNCIL: IMPLICATIONS FOR CITIZENSHIP

- The school council provides an exercise in democracy at the tutor/year group and school levels.

- Pupils participate in choosing representatives.

- Some will themselves participate in debate and decision-making and all will have demonstrated to them the need for formal ways of resolving disputes and legislating or creating rules.

CHAPTER 4

THE ELECTION OF SCHOOL OFFICERS

Context

There are few things less attractive to a teenager than the procedural details of the parliamentary system and few things more exciting than participation in decision-making. It follows, therefore, that young people will understand democratic processes and appreciate democratic responsibilities much more if they can be part of them rather than being taught about them.

The practice of democratic representation can become part of the school culture, whether voting for year council delegates, representatives of house or charity groups or school officers. Elections for school officers need to take place with due formality and detail. Candidates should be given clear guidelines on presentation and appropriate tactics before they are asked to explain to the electorate – the pupil body – why they are the right people for the job. They should answer probing questions during the campaign and gather support. In our experience they often do this with an energy that would put many an MP to shame!

School officers are the most senior pupils elected to represent the pupil body in meetings with the head teacher, school leadership or management team, pupils from other schools and at numerous school evening functions.

Election of school officers – the people

Before anyone considers putting himself or herself forward for a position as one of the school officers there is a need to understand, at least in outline, what the role involves. A useful first step is to set out the roles, responsibilities, required behaviour and characteristics in a school diary or some other easily accessible place. Clearly, these roles will vary depending on the school involved but a useful, if somewhat traditional, list is:

- School officers who work as a team:

    - *head boy;*

    - *head girl;*

    - *deputy head boy;*

    - *deputy head girl;*

    - *chair of the charity committee;*

    - *deputy chair of the charity committee.*

- Internal roles carried out within the school and encompassing a wide range of tasks:

    - *leadership of the 'whole school community' and membership of the school council;*

    - *provision of advice to head teacher and school management team.*

- External roles which confer a high profile on these pupils in the wider community:

    - *assisting at parents' conferences and other school and social functions;*

    - *helping with press and public relations.*

- Required characteristics:

    - *creativity to produce new ideas and methods;*

    - *reactivity to seek and represent views;*

    - *leadership to generate enthusiasm, listening skills;*

    - *responsibility to carry out tasks properly and on time;*

    - *effectiveness to form plans and organize others.*

Having assessed themselves against this checklist, the sensible potential candidates will also wish to discuss the role with the officers currently in post.

Chair and deputy chair of the charity committee

It is worth looking in more detail at the role of two particular school officers, the chair and deputy chair of the charity committee. These are key roles involving overall management, drafting of agendas and chairing meetings around charity events. With this comes the following:

- *Internal responsibilities:*
    - *liaison with school management team;*
    - *liaison with support staff;*
    - *liaison with head of year and teaching staff;*
    - *reports to school council;*
    - *effective communication with pupils.*

- *External responsibilities:*
    - *liaison with chosen charity/charities;*
    - *liaison with retailers, local business;*
    - *liaison with local celebrity and media.*

- *Qualities:*
    - *commitment;*
    - *enthusiasm;*
    - *reliability;*
    - *effective communication;*
    - *calmness under pressure;*
    - *creativity;*
    - *organization.*

Much of this will be explained further in the context of the charity fashion show described in Chapter 6.

The chair of the charity committee is leader of the charity team comprised of a range of posts such as treasurer, secretary, publicity manager, stage manager and choreographer (these last two posts are specifically relevant to the fashion show).

Election of school officers – the process

Nomination

Once the appropriate research has been carried out the pupils who wish to stand in the elections need to attract a nomination. In order to do this they need to convince their year group peers to nominate them. Potential candidates are usually the most senior pupils in the school and so have behind them evidence of their contribution to the school over preceding years. This, alongside their peers' understanding of their personal qualities, should be the guide for nominators. Once nominations have been agreed a nomination paper is completed. The key points to note for the nomination paper are:

- there has to be a proposer and seconder;

- each nomination is for a particular post;

- there has to be acceptance of the nomination by the named candidate;

- there is an understanding that the candidate will serve in the capacity of deputy to the nominated post if they come second in the election.

As in national and local elections there are strict requirements that should be adhered to at every stage.

Statement of intent

Each candidate has to produce a statement outlining why he or she is the right person for the role. They must convince the electorate that they have the skills and qualities needed and will be a good leader and ambassador for the school.

The statement should be limited in size (say 150 words); there will be a wide variety of approaches among the statements produced.

The statements should be distributed at various points throughout the school so that all pupils have access to them. They should also be circulated to school staff. The candidates should eventually present their statements to pupils personally during the election. This can be done through assemblies.

Voting

Every pupil within the school and every member of staff, teaching and support, has a single vote. The polling stations, which are open for a full day, are located in the staff centre/room (for staff) and in an easily accessible classroom for pupils.

Counting

This is carried out by a member of staff in the presence of the current school officers. This will be the last duty they perform in their school officer role.

Announcement of successful candidates

The names of successful candidates are posted on noticeboards and announced in assemblies once the results have been made known to all the candidates.

School officers – the responsibilities in practice

As has been indicated above, the roles and responsibilities of the school officers are many and varied. Below is a possible list of the tasks they may have to undertake:

- Front of house at open or parents' evenings. They are there to meet and greet parents and guests. The school officers hand out programmes, give directions and answer questions as necessary.

- Attendance at induction events for incoming Year 7 pupils. The school officers make a verbal input into the evening, being introduced to parents alongside key members of staff, outlining their responsibilities and giving their candid impression of the school. They also work directly with Year 7 pupils.

- Regular meetings with the head teacher. Here there is the opportunity for the school officers to make a direct input into policy making by arguing issues on behalf of the body of pupils.

- Involvement in year assemblies. The first assembly they should, perhaps, attend is the one at the beginning of the year, to introduce themselves and give assurances about their accessibility.

- Representation of the school at meetings of senior pupils from all schools in the Education Authority area.

- Representation and leadership on the senior year council.

Conclusion

The system described has been proved to work. Of course, pupils do not all agree on the direction of desirable change. Their suggestions cannot always be implemented but they do know that their opinions are valued and sought after. They do have the opportunity to vote for their representatives and recognize a collective responsibility for many areas of school life. They know that decisions are made after consultation and that feedback is always given.

Other elections

The above model could be used for a mock election, timed to coincide with local, national or European elections. The candidates, rather than standing for particular posts, could represent the major (and perhaps some fringe) political parties. The statements would be their personal and party's manifesto, produced after suitable research in order to ensure realism. Publicity could be used with posters, flyers, leaflets, etc. The election in this case becomes a mirror of the external political process and can be used in a wide variety of ways, in and out of the classroom, to stimulate political and moral, social and environmental awareness.

ELECTIONS OF SCHOOL OFFICERS: IMPLICATIONS FOR CITIZENSHIP

- Clearly the similarities between the process described here and local and national elections are easy to explain. Those involved in the election process, in any capacity, learn about the legal and human rights underpinning society and how they relate to citizens.

- They begin to recognize the importance of playing an active part in democratic and electoral processes.

- Those directly involved as candidates will learn how to research a topical political, moral, social or cultural issue by analysing information from different sources and be able to express, justify and defend a personal opinion about issues, problems and events.

- Everyone involved will learn to contribute to group and exploratory class discussions and take part in formal debates.

- Specifically, those participating as candidates will be able to consider other people's experiences and be able to think about and express views that are not their own.

PART 3

WHOLE-SCHOOL ACTIVITIES

CHAPTER 5

INTRODUCING A SCHOOL FESTIVAL OR ACTIVITIES WEEK

The purpose of a festival

A school festival is an event, organized over several days, involving all the staff and pupils in a range of activities and events that are unusual or different from the normal school routine. These events are aimed at giving pupils experiences not normally available within the school or in their day-to-day lives and could be adventurous, charitable, sporting, tasters for new subjects, competitions, exploratory or research based or working in the community. The range of possible activities is very wide.

A festival will necessitate the suspension of the taught National Curriculum for a few days in favour of an activities week or festival celebration. It will give the opportunity for everyone in the school to become involved in different ways in meeting aims for themselves, for the school and for the community. A number of the concepts and required outcomes identified in citizenship can also be addressed by a festival in ways different from those normally followed in a taught lesson. A festival can also assist the achievement of key skills and address PSHE issues whilst at the same time provide developmental opportunities and enjoyment through a variety of events and activities. Care must be taken, however, to ensure that the festival does not become simply a 'fun week'. Clearly there is a huge potential for fun for all participants but this does not have to be at the expense of developmental and educational opportunities.

It is suggested that staff are invited to put forward activities that they would be happy to organize or lead. The variety of activities on offer could include giving more time to the current extracurricular activities as well as exciting new and different activities that will capture the imagination of pupils. Many of the activities on offer should hit citizenship targets, key skills and aims of the school.

Festival organization and rationale

For most schools the best time for the curriculum to be collapsed will be at the end of the academic year. Year 11 will have left and there is additional non-contact time for staff available. Also many schemes of work will have reached their natural conclusion for the year or key stage. The festival has to be an integral part of the school year and, in many ways, it can be seen as the culmination of best practice in citizenship and other fields. The festival needs to demonstrate citizenship in action to all and to facilitate learning about the key principles of citizenship. Experience of running an annual school festival has shown that it is possible to achieve some or all of the following goals that are relevant:

- the promotion of personal and social development enabling pupils to become more self-confident in and beyond the classroom;

- an understanding by pupils/students that a fair method of selection for activities is operated and that no guarantee of preferred choices is offered;

- an equality of provision that does not prevent any pupil/student from participating in an activity on the grounds of cost.

Communication is, therefore, the key to the successful involvement of all concerned and needs to be full, frank and transparent. Known and agreed procedures based upon democratic decision-making are important for the smooth working of the festival.

It is not always possible, obviously, for all pupils to have their first choices of activities on all days and a system of prioritization should be used based on specific year groups. Whether or not a computerized system is used to identify pupils for activities, the system chosen must be seen to be fair. There need to be clear guidelines and the following are generally seen to promote fairness:

- all pupils go on the appropriate year trip;

- pupils choose first, second and third preferences for each day;

- each year has priority for one day;

- when an activity is oversubscribed, the year with priority for the day is given places ensuring as many as possible get their first choice; any remaining available places are allocated through a random selection (names in a hat or a random-selection computer program);

- when the numbers in the priority year choosing an activity exceeds the numbers of available places, the random selection process is used for this selection too.

Nevertheless, there will be disappointments for some and disappointed pupils can be reminded of the democratic nature of the decisions made.

Possible activities

Within the festival/activities week there are a number of events that can be included. In most activities the key skills involved are clearly identifiable and from this the corresponding citizenship knowledge, skills and understanding can be identified. The following is by no means an exhaustive list but it does give a flavour of what pupils can learn and represents a selection of activities that have been successfully used.

- Animation workshop – an introduction to video animation and associated 2D and 3D techniques. Working in small groups pupils produce their own video sequence, first planning with a storyboard, then making the models and artwork, and finally the animation is recorded on video.

- Camping – a chance for pupils to fend for themselves for 24 hours, to camp in a forest campsite and to look for forest wildlife including birds, bats and owls.

- Climbing – pupils train in an indoor sport climbing centre with expert tuition.

- Conservation workshop – a chance for pupils to do some hands-on conservation in the local area. Activities might include pond clearing, path building, hedge laying and creating wildlife areas.

- Create a soap opera – pupils are invited to build their own version (of the 'Street' or 'Square') and become their own character with a secret past and a stormy future!

- Drama workshop – pupils are encouraged to make the world a better place while having lots of fun working with a professional sustainable development group. Pupils could be involved in a creative session with an environmental theme.

- Egg drop – working in pairs or small groups, pupils design and build safe methods of transport for raw eggs that are to be dropped from great heights.

- Historical trail – pupils are given the opportunity to find out about local history and to be a historical detective for an afternoon investigating local historical clues. These can be from any period in history.

- Japanese for beginners – pupils are given an introduction to Japanese language and culture.

- Jazz dance workshop – pupils work with a professional dancer and actress in an energetic and funky jazz dance workshop.

- Makaton workshop – pupils learn to use Makaton, a sign language which is a simpler form of British Sign Language used to communicate with people with special educational needs/physical disabilities. Learning is through activities and video materials.

- Publish a Web Page – pupils learn to make their own Internet pages, scan pictures and surf the net.

- Rocket science for beginners – the opportunity for pupils to find out what makes rockets fly. They build, prepare and launch hydraulic (water) and pyrotechnic (chemical) rockets and experience what it is like to be a rocket scientist for a day. Tuition is under the guidance of an expert from higher education.

- Theatre visit – pupils are given the opportunity to see behind the scenes at a local theatre. Also involved is a drama workshop.

Other suggestions

- Year trips to encourage team building and communication within a year group (ie the whole year goes on the trip) visiting local places of historical interest, a theme park, an environmental location or a trip further afield, to a major city perhaps.

- Personal development workshops – designed to meet the needs of a specific year group. This could be particularly applicable to a school with a sixth form where application for universities, colleges and employment could be addressed. Sample UCAS forms could be completed or employment portfolios updated. Computer facilities could be on hand for CV writing, etc.

There are many other activities that could be offered, using the expertise of both teaching and support staff on site, or by liaising with local firms or organizations.

There are many opportunities to run events similar to these described without associating them with a festival. Clearly these would need to be tailored to the needs and environment of the individual school. Taking the opportunity to create a festival does, however, reduce the workload and distraction of running such events during the normal school timetable and programme.

SCHOOL FESTIVAL: IMPLICATIONS FOR CITIZENSHIP

- The success of the festival in achieving knowledge about citizenship depends on a thorough review and analysis of what happened, what was achieved and what were the issues that arose. Care must be taken to extract as much learning as possible about the fundamental strands of citizenship education.

- Pupils will gain an appreciation of democracy in action relating to issues of choice of activities, limitations, expectations, etc.

- They will recognize that evaluation can and will affect future festivals.

- They will begin to appreciate that rights and responsibilities are linked together.

- Pupils in unfamiliar situations should be allowed to take responsibility for their own actions and appreciate the trust shown in them by supporting adults.

- There will be changes in the relationship between adults and pupils as the organization of the festival proceeds and this should give an insight into roles and responsibilities in relationships.

CHAPTER 6

RUNNING A CHARITY EVENT

In most schools, it is probable that charities are supported within the year by various groups of pupils and events. This may be through activities such as a non-uniform day, a charity week, a school sale or fair, a performance with part of the proceeds going to a named charity or involvement in a national organization day such as the Poppy Appeal, Comic Relief, Children in Need. A charity event can be arranged for any time of the year or included in a festival/activities week and is, in many ways, a natural extension of the on-going involvement by people in the school in charity work. A high-profile charity event will encourage pupils to become even more helpfully involved in the life of their school and the community and provide assistance for a charity. Pupils can, thus, be given the opportunity to demonstrate personal and corporate responsibility in their attitude to others, their school and the local community.

RUNNING A LOCAL CHARITY EVENT: IMPLICATIONS FOR CITIZENSHIP

- Pupils practise skills of negotiation in order to reach agreement about the most appropriate activities to provide and they are involved in the research and planning of a range of activities suitable for elderly people with limited mobility, and so contribute to group and exploratory discussions.

- Pupils are involved with part of the external community and have to take note of that group's specific needs and learn to appreciate the diversity of needs.

In this chapter some examples of work that have been done in this area are described and the learning about citizenship that is possible from such work is outlined.

Another example of an event that can be run on a regular basis is an annual fashion show. The format we describe below does not, of course, have to be followed slavishly but can be used as a prompt for your own local action.

CASE STUDY: THE LOCAL CHARITY

Pupils were asked to identify an appropriate local charity which would benefit from involvement of the school. They were also asked to identify appropriate activities which they were then expected to plan and run. In this particular case, a number of elderly people's homes were approached with a view to providing an afternoon of refreshment and entertainment for their residents on the school site. Pupils used their imagination and carried out some research to ensure that the experience provided would be an appropriate one for the guests. This research covered such issues as:

- provision of appropriate dietary requirements;

- provision of comfortable surroundings and adequate facilities (including those for people with limited mobility);

- suitable methods of entertainment and how to provide it – this resulted in a bingo session, a sing-song and a display of dance routines;

- exploration into the logistics of transporting the elderly.

The project provided many opportunities to promote mutual respect and understanding. It was a joy to see a 13-year-old boy in the role of bingo caller, having learnt all the terminology, responding to the repartee of experienced bingo players. The different generations singing pre- and post-war songs together bridged the age gap in a way that history lessons rarely can. Similarly, the enjoyment of the elderly watching young people dance to modern songs was evidence of the fact that age was no barrier to mutual respect and understanding.

The fashion show

Background

The fashion show is a positive way in which to raise money for local and national charities, involving the school and the wider community and allowing pupils to demonstrate organizational, financial, interpersonal and creative skills. As much as possible, input on these issues should come from pupils and as time progresses there should be less and less close direction from staff.

Fashion show organization

The venue for the fashion show is the school, the models are school pupils and other children from the local community, the outfits are provided by local shops and the publicity, lighting and choreography are the responsibility of the pupils. The fashion show traditionally runs on two evenings and there are four compères, usually senior pupils or school officers; they are responsible for their scripts, introducing models, acknowledging shops and making the links between the appearance of each of the models on stage. Several teams are involved and each team has 3–4 minutes on stage, during which they model the clothes and perform a choreographed routine to suitable music. The show is in two parts with an interval and compères change over at the interval. It is a very demanding activity. It is also time-consuming but the benefits, which are more than simply financial, are tremendous.

The organizing committee

The pupils who are the powerhouse behind the fashion show are the school's charity committee. They choose the charities to benefit from the proceeds of the event. This is done democratically, the only proviso being that there should be one local and one national charity. A vote is ultimately taken, but if a member of the committee has a personal reason for supporting a particular charity they have a powerful forum in which to argue in favour of that charity.

The chosen charities are contacted, so that their name and logo can be used on any publicity material, and they are invited to become more closely involved in the fashion show. This closer involvement can take many forms; the charity may donate prizes for a raffle held in the interval or articles for decorating the hall and stage. They may help with the printing of tickets or leaflets or send a representative to talk briefly about the work of the charity at the beginning of the fashion show. From our experience, however, the involvement that pupils found very satisfying and most rewarding was when the local branch of an organization for the physically handicapped was supported and some of the children with disabilities come on stage to model outfits.

Groups with devolved responsibilities

The task of organizing a fashion show is huge and teamwork is the only way in which it can be accomplished. In order that it does not become overwhelming, the chair of the charity committee and other members seek help and support. Pupils sign up to be models, choreographers, stage builders, backstage helpers, front of house, technical/lighting experts, publicists and so on. Groups are constructed from the list of volunteers and it is the responsibility of these groups to organize their area of input. One individual is appointed as shop liaison officer with responsibility for co-ordinating all the information about the outfits on loan, counting the clothes into school, looking after them while they are there and then counting them out again. The Fashion Show Shop Allocation Form (Figure 6.1) should be helpful.

The roles of the groups are briefly as follows:

- *Choreography team.* Each group of pupils who will model the clothes also has to devise a routine to music in order to show off the clothes to their best advantage. They may seek the help of choreographers from the senior dance club.

- *Production team.* Pupils in the production team are responsible for selecting the theme of the evening; they build the set and plan the decoration of the hall according to that theme. They also liaise with other groups to ensure that the publicity leaflets, colour scheme and tickets tie in with the theme.

- *Publicity team.* Once the theme has been decided the publicity team swings into action to produce the leaflets, programmes and tickets. They liaise with art classes, the school's resources team and local press.

FASHION SHOW SHOP ALLOCATION FORM

Pupil group: _____

Shop: _____

Address: _____

Contact: _____

Telephone No: _____

The above shop has been allocated to you for the fashion show. Please 'phone the shop, ask to speak to the contact and arrange for a time to visit them to find the clothes that you will be modelling.

Attached to this letter is a form in duplicate. Fill this in with the manager of the shop and return one to us after your visit. The second copy needs to stay with the manager. It is important, for insurance purposes, that these forms are filled out correctly.

YOU MUST NOT TAKE ANY CLOTHES AWAY WITH YOU WHEN YOU VISIT THE SHOP AS THEY WILL NOT BE COVERED BY INSURANCE UNTIL THEY ARE COLLECTED FOR THE SHOW.

If you experience any problems with the shop please let us know and we will contact them.

School contact name and number: _____

Figure 6.1 Fashion show shop allocation form

■ *Technical crew*. Lighting and music have to be sympathetic to the work of the models on stage; lighting and sound at all technical rehearsals and throughout the fashion show itself are the responsibility of the technical crew.

Liaison with shops

Which shops should be involved?

A variety of shops can be involved in and support the fashion show. It may be interesting to note that the larger fashion/retail outlets are often less willing to become involved in the project. Contact has to been made with major nationwide companies. They may be supportive of the idea but it may be rare that this support is translated into practical help. On the whole the shops represented will tend to be local and perhaps smaller outlets. The agreement with the shops should be that they will loan to the fashion show a number of outfits that will be modelled on stage, with full acknowledgement of their support and a positive plug for the shop concerned. The number of outfits each shop loans could vary from just one or two to double figures.

What are their concerns?

Clearly, the shops involved will want to make sure that their input is recognized and valued. The organizers must ensure that loans and support are fully acknowledged. Supporters are also, naturally, very concerned about the care that will be taken of their outfits and look for guarantees that they will be returned in the same condition they were loaned. In order to provide reassurance on this point, an insurance policy should be taken out to cover the cost of any damage or loss (Figure 6.2). This is negotiated by the pupils with the finance officer. The pupils also ensure that there is a named person who liaises with each shop and so builds up a trust with that organization. The paperwork should also give reassurance. Each shop completes a form giving full details of the clothes borrowed, the name of the contact, details of the school, etc (see Figure 6.1). There is also a letter of authorization from the school assuring that the venture is *bona fide*!

What outfits can be loaned?

A variety of outfits can be loaned. They can range through casual, formal, evening and sports wear. Each year the fashion show can have a theme and so the clothes can be chosen to fit in with this theme.

FASHION SHOW LOAN LIST

WE HAVE INSURANCE TO COVER ANY OCCURRENCE.

Pupil group: _____

Shop: _____

Telephone no: _____

We will collect clothes on .... and return them on ....
Please keep a record below of the clothes that you are lending us along with the value for insurance purposes.

Product description/Code number	Size	Colour	Value

Number of garments loaned [   ]
Total value [   ]

Figure 6.2 Fashion show loan list

Who will be the models?

Although most of the models will be older pupils in the school, a few members of the community can be included each year. These might be younger pupils from partner primary schools, representatives from local charities or younger children of staff at the school. Both male and female models should be well represented; there have been some teams of all boy models.

Themes

A variety of themes can be used for the fashion show. Once a theme is decided upon, then the stage set, decoration and all publicity, along with the music, the outfits and compères' scripts have to develop this theme and link together all of the models to promote the unity of the theme. Some suggested themes are:

- 'The Big Day'. Here the finale of each half of the show is a wedding party with the 'brides' in outfits ranging from the traditional white 'meringue' to shepherdess-style dresses, the grooms in a range of suits from top hat and tails to a very casual outfit and bridesmaids to suit the theme, with dresses for both very tiny bridesmaids (and pages) and teenage bridesmaids.

- 'A Night Out'. This may feature the huge range of attire favoured by the rich and famous (or would-be so!) at the presentation of awards. It may include a number of performances based on films, *Bond 007* films for example.

- 'Sixties and Seventies'. This could look at the resurrection of clothes seen in the era of Woodstock and earlier.

The finishing touches

In the scale of this production the finishing touches, and perhaps the less glamorous aspects of good organization, should not be overlooked. These provide great opportunities for wide involvement of pupils in the event. The charity committee also has to ensure that there are pupils ready to undertake such things as:

- liaising with the caretaking and cleaning staff in order to minimize disruption and to ensure that the hall is not left in an untidy state after the productions;

- ensuring the clothes are picked up and returned on time – here a team of drivers is needed and the pupils exercise their skills influencing parents and staff;

- looking after young models who may have to wait between their appearances on stage and ensuring they turn up for their cue on time and looking their best;

- ensuring there are helpers to provide safety pins, do hair, check the hang of a dress, find that missing shoe, etc;

- providing refreshments (again fitting in with the theme!) at the interval, for guests and also for models.

Suggestions for expansion

There are a number of ways in which the interval can be used to further increase funds for charity or to extend the scope of the evening. Some of those listed below have been tried and tested, others are merely suggestions. Many more developments could be introduced.

- An 'allied' business could be invited to become involved. For example, a cosmetics company could come to the fashion show and give out promotional tickets, offering say 10 per cent off make-up, to be used at a local department store. A pupil could be given a full make-up during the interval and visitors could watch. The make-up company give a donation for the chosen charity.

- A local celebrity, preferably one with links to the chosen charity, could say a few words at the end of the first half of the show and donate some possession to be raffled during the interval.

- A raffle could be held of items donated by organizations, parents and other supporters.

■ Information relating to the relevant charities could be viewed during the interval; charities may wish to set up information stands or show a video for people to spend a few minutes watching.

THE FASHION SHOW: IMPLICATIONS FOR CITIZENSHIP

■ Pupils involved in the fashion show, in any capacity, learn about the responsibilities underpinning society and how they relate to citizens.

■ They begin to recognize the importance of playing an active part in democratic and electoral processes.

■ They also begin to become aware of how the economy functions, including the role of business and financial services.

■ Those involved learn how to research a topical issue by analysing information.

■ They learn how to express and justify opinions and become involved in group discussions, and put all this into practice.

■ Pupils learn about the work of local, national or international charities and the opportunities that individuals have to bring about social change.

CHAPTER 7

SETTING UP A DEBATING SOCIETY

Participating in debate is a fine opportunity for pupils to experience the democratic process in action. Not only are moral and social issues researched, considered and expressed but the participants are also exposed to opinions and beliefs that are different from their own. Debate encourages participation, it hones reasoning and communication skills, and it mirrors parliamentary and democratic procedures. A useful resource for this chapter is *The Sport of Debating: Winning skills and strategies* by Phillips and Hooke.

The value of ritual behaviour

Pupils and students get a quite unexpected thrill from following the 'rules' of debating. It is not at all uncommon to find that the imposition of agreed behaviour restraints and the role-playing that goes with it encourages previously quiet members of a class to voice subtle and unsuspected views. The focus that formality offers will also serve to raise concentration levels and engender articulate, thoughtful debate. Debating is *not* arguing.

The differing roles of debaters

There are three main types of participant in a debate:

- the chairperson;

- the speakers (for and against);

- the floor.

Each category needs to get a very real chance to participate. The roles are as follows:

- The *chairperson* is in charge of the debate, calling on each of the speakers to speak and opening up debate to the floor when the time comes. It is their job to maintain order and see to it that the formality of the occasion is preserved. A lot of pupils and students want to perform this role because of the implicit power it confers, but the best chairpersons are those who use their power to facilitate the discussion; this is a useful lesson for all.

- The *speakers* set the debate in motion by providing arguments for their position on the issue in question. It is normal to have two speakers for each side though more or less are quite admissible. Speaking is quite daunting for most pupils and students and not only because of the immediate demands of addressing their peers. The best speeches are the result of good research rather than off-the-cuff retorts and this requires an extra level of dedication. The speeches may last anywhere from one to seven minutes.

- The *floor* consists of all those members of the class or debating society or 'house' who are not otherwise occupied. When the chairperson opens the debate up to the floor (see below) individual members of the floor may question the speakers when recognized by the chairperson.

It is also quite usual to have a third speaker for either side who will summarize the major points made during debate and give a vote of thanks to all those involved.

Basic procedure of debating

1. The room

Have the chairperson seated behind a desk or table at one end of the room. The speakers are on either side of the chairperson with those proposing the motion to the right, those opposing it to the left. The 'floor' is then made up of individuals seated facing the chairperson and speakers. In this arrangement the floor is neutral, although it is possible to have a 'team' arrangement where the floor is made up of two sides each sitting on the side of 'their' speakers and ready to participate in a parliamentary fashion, asking questions to support their own 'team'.

2. The chairperson brings the 'house' to order

A formal procedure deserves a formal opening and the chairperson will do this by calling for silence.

3. The motion is read out

Whatever the subject under debate is to be, eg 'This house believes the printed book is dying', it needs stating before debate begins.

4. The speakers are introduced by name, and as either proposer or opposer

It is also important to state who will be the primary and who the secondary speaker.

5. The rules of debate are highlighted

It may sound very silly, but all speech of any kind must be prefaced by the words 'Mr/Madam Chair and members of the floor'. This is to ensure order and perhaps to allow the possibly overheated debater the chance to regain some self-control. If any debater should forget this prologue, then the chairperson should demand correction immediately. It actually makes for a lot of fun when pupils see one another behaving in this way! Another formality which participants enjoy is that each debater is only allowed to begin speaking (and hence utter the words outlined above) once the chairperson has indicated that they may begin to speak by saying '[Debater's name] you have been recognized'.

6. The chairperson calls on the primary proposition speaker

This speaker should endeavour to set limits to the motion, defining their understanding of it and discussing key arguments. A good structure for all speakers is to have three clear points that are signposted before they are discussed, when they are discussed and after they have been discussed.

7. The chairperson calls on the primary opposition speaker

This speaker needs to have done a similar amount of preparation as the primary proposition speaker but must be prepared to be flexible should the proposition speaker have introduced something unexpected or which the opposition speaker wishes to challenge.

8. The chairperson calls on the secondary proposition speaker

9. The chairperson calls on the secondary opposition speaker

Both secondary speakers develop the arguments of their respective side but need to be alert for opportunities to think on their feet and rebut their opponents' arguments.

10. The chairperson thanks all speakers and opens the debate to the floor

This should be the longest section of the entire debate. The members of the floor are encouraged to raise their hands if they wish to speak and are 'recognized' by the chairperson in as fair a rotation as possible. The members of the floor must endeavour to phrase all points they have as questions to one or more of the speakers. In this way, simple statements of belief are transformed into the kind of discourse which will clarify and lead to further discussion of the issues.

11. When a set time has elapsed the chairperson brings the debate to a close

It is normally best to set a 'guillotine time', say 20 minutes, for the floor debate. The chairperson may decide it is necessary to extend the time allowed if interest and other time pressures permit. It is common to discover that the debate will 'hot up' as time goes on and it can be a shame to curtail it arbitrarily. On the other hand, should the floor debate have difficulties getting going it is the chairperson's job to stimulate ideas and ask questions.

12. The chairperson calls on each summarizer to speak

The summarizers will give their account of the most salient points made and then thank all who have taken part. This is quite a skilled task and requires very good listening skills.

13. The chairperson thanks each summarizer and moves to voting procedure

When voting, it is only necessary for the chairperson to ask those in favour to raise their hands and then those against. There should be no 'party line' to follow; each vote should be a direct result of the debate and the points made. The motion will then be either carried or defeated. This is the formal close of the debate.

Getting started

A debating society should be organized to meet at appropriate intervals; once a week during a lunchtime works well. There can be certain issues to consider if starting from scratch. Having all age groups arrive for the first session with none of them knowing what to do is not a good move. Instead, start with a more senior year group, Year 12 or 10/11 depending on the school, and train them up. Their debates should be public. Once they are sufficiently experienced you can ask them to construct assemblies to publicize junior debating societies for younger members of the school or gradually absorb a wider audience from among those who have observed proceedings. The older, more experienced, debaters can help to organize and support younger debaters although adult supervision is appreciated by all concerned to begin with.

The following points should be considered when setting up your debating society.

- Have an initial publicity assembly where, perhaps with the aid of some drama students, you demonstrate the difference between arguing and debating and some of the joys of formalized discussion.

- If possible, secure a debating society noticeboard on which you can advertise forthcoming debates including the names of the chairperson and speakers.

- Allow as much time for the debate itself as possible; remember things normally hot up as they go on. It may be appropriate to allow those attending at a lunchtime debate, for instance, to eat in your debating room.

- Give solid instructions to your first round of speakers. Tell them to research for facts that they can understand and interpret, brainstorm for ideas and deliver a three-point speech that satisfies the function of their role (see earlier). Try to allow at least a week for them to prepare. Begin with one-minute speeches and extend as your debaters become more practised.

- Members of staff can chair debates in the early days to ensure the correct use of procedures and to encourage the less voluble to speak. When pupils have contributed once they are usually less shy. This is good for all.

- Don't neglect the vote; students always want to see what other people think.

- When the society is healthily established invite other interest groups to debate with you, eg Christian Union, PE students, budding scientists, staff, etc.

Skills to teach debaters

You cannot simply let the debating ball roll and hope it will find direction on its own; debating skills need to be learnt. It is best to make skills acquisition experiential rather than a function of classes in rhetoric. The following list suggests ways you can start to address the skills required.

- Brainstorm as many arguments for and against the motion as possible; it always pays to try and second-guess the opposition.

- When saying anything, structure it so that it can be clearly understood by a listener. Chaotic utterances are the easiest to rebut or ignore.

- Speakers should try to order their speech into three main points. Listening is difficult, so tell us what you're going to say, tell us what you are telling us then tell us what you've told us. We might get it then.

- When responding to a speech or question, try to summarize your understanding of the opponent's point before giving your own. This will encourage listening skills, limit unfocused responses and help keep the debate on track.

- Investigate how body language and use of eye contact influence an audience. Think about tone and pace of voice and how it varies at appropriate moments to keep an audience interested and show them the most crucial points.

- The 'point of information' is an incredibly useful tool but only to be introduced once debating is well understood. During speeches or even questions from the floor any member of the house can stand up and say 'on a point of information', and it is then up to the speaker at the time if they wish to accept what this person has to say; if they do then they risk having a thorny question to answer there and then. Points of information can be requests for clarification or further information, offering a fact that disproves what has just been said or pointing out a contradiction in the argument. As such the point of information can be a powerful aid to listening skills and a genuine motivator for logical and analytical engagement with ideas. Don't allow too many and don't allow them on a speaker's debut.

Moving the debate outside the school

There are plenty of opportunities for your debating society to engage in activities outside the school:

- Friendly debates with other schools.

- Debating and public speaking competitions run by various organizations.

- Attending a model 'United Nations' event. These are organized nationally and internationally and attract large numbers of students. Information can be obtained from the United Nations Association of the UK (www.una-uk.org). A team of your students assumes the role of one of the world's nations and has to argue and make policy decisions based on their political and diplomatic outlook. These events are a great learning experience and a lot of fun. They are held regularly in a variety of locations.

- Visits to see the workings of local, central or devolved seats of government, the courts, etc.

- Community involvement with local charitable organizations, democratic associations, pressure groups, etc. All these offer grounds for good research if not specifically for debate.

- Inviting outside speakers in to speak and 'receive questions'.

A list of possible debating motions is set out in Table 7.1.

Table 7.1 Cross-curricular debates*

Key Stage	English	Modern languages	History	Science	Religious education	Geography
3	'Advertising is just for fun'	'English should be the global language'	'History is best forgotten'	'Scientists are dangerous people'	'Religion is only important for people in poor countries'	'Roads are more important than parks'
4	'All regional accents should be banned'	'Foreign languages are easy – even footballers can learn them'	'There is no such thing as privacy in the modern state'	'Scientists do not help society advance'	'Euthanasia should be part of a civilized society' 'Marriage is an outdated concept'	'No new houses should be built in Britain'
5	'Films are more important than books'	'Language equals culture'	'History judges a culture by the way it treats minorities'	'Rape is a natural biological process'	'Buildings are the god of institutional religion'	'Maps are more important than the places they represent'

* All motions for debate need to be prefaced with the phrase 'This house believes that ...'. Other ideas can be obtained from *Pros and Cons* published by The English Speaking Union.

THE DEBATING SOCIETY: IMPLICATIONS FOR CITIZENSHIP

- Participation in debate is a core requirement of citizenship. The formality of a debating society provides an excellent opportunity for pupils to practise the art of influencing others through the force of argument.

- The cut and thrust of the debate hones communication and reasoning skills.

- The obvious similarities between the debate in school and those in parliament can be readily shown. Few other activities involve skills of enquiry and communication or those of participation so intensely.

- The practice of debate allows pupils to experience first hand how issues are dealt with in a political forum.

- Political literacy is almost a self-generating by-product of the range of motions debated. No debater can really engage with the issues without discovering who thinks what and why. Desire to understand the issues, to outwit an opponent or to give a good account of themselves produces the curiosity which underpins all good learning experiences.

- A successful debating society can dispel apathy and increase commitment to democratic change.

- In addition, people with strong opinions learn to consider that differing viewpoints might be legitimate and that disagreement is not an assault on one's own identity. Debating, after all, is designed to make you think harder about what you believe you already know; it is a vital tool in making sense of citizenship.

CHAPTER 8

HUMAN RIGHTS: A RELIGIOUS EDUCATION OR PHILOSOPHY AND BELIEF DAY

The following example of a one-day philosophy and belief conference illustrates one innovative way in which the social and moral responsibility strand of citizenship at Key Stage 4 might be delivered. (*Note:* the day conference approach requires a suspension of the normal timetable to allow a whole year group to participate in a series of workshops throughout the day.)

'Whose life is it anyway?'

Aims: A conference to research, consider and debate the issue of euthanasia in the context of human rights.

Workshop 1, Human rights

Introduction

This first workshop of the day is intended to explore the issue of human rights in general. It starts by looking at what it might be like to experience the denial of a significant right. An example of this might be the loss of freedom suffered by an innocent person. Brian Keenan was one such person who was held hostage in Beirut for four and a half years. Start the workshop with a dramatic reading of extracts from *An Evil Cradling*, his book written to describe his experiences. A good section to use is in Chapter 5, 'Jailhouse Rock' pp. 35–37. Pupils are then asked to describe in writing one powerful image from the reading. Through discussion, pupils identify those factors which affected the quality of Brian Keenan's life and the basic human rights that he was denied.

Development

In small groups pupils participate in a discussion to prioritize a list of human rights, featuring examples taken from the Universal Declaration of Human Rights which includes, for example, the right to freedom of speech, to communicate with family and the right not to be tortured (see Table 8.1).

This is followed up immediately by a discussion of which rights were the most highly/least highly valued and why. Pupils identify any fundamental rights that they consider to be the entitlement of all humans.

IMPLICATIONS FOR CITIZENSHIP

Pupils are encouraged to reflect on those rights that they consider to be important in their own lives.

Table 8.1 Human rights

In your groups prioritize this list of human rights. Categorize them as one of the following:

A. of the greatest importance;
B. of great significance;
C. very important;
D. important but not essential;
E. nice to have but not of real significance.

No.	Right	Priority
1.	Everyone has the right to medical care	
2.	Everyone has the right to education	
3.	Everyone has the right to read the papers	
4.	Everyone has the right to a nutritious diet	
5.	Everyone has the right to clothing	
6.	Everyone has the right to clean water	
7.	Everyone has the right to freedom of thought and to express their opinion both privately and in public	
8.	Everyone has the right to mental health and not to be kept in solitary confinement	
9.	Everyone has the right not to be killed	
10.	Everyone has the right to communicate freely with their family	
11.	Everyone has the right to self-defence	
12.	Everyone has the right to work in safe and healthy conditions	
13.	Everyone has the right to be free from unjust interference in their family, home, privacy and correspondence	
14.	Everyone has the right not to be discriminated against on the grounds of race or religion	
15.	Everyone has the right to equal pay for equal work	
16.	Everyone has the right to own property	

continued overleaf

Table 8.1 continued

No.	Right	Priority
17.	Everyone has the right to rest and leisure, including reasonable working hours and holidays with pay	
18.	Everyone has the right to be assumed innocent until proven guilty	
19.	Everyone, whether man or woman, has the right to equal rights in marriage and divorce	
20.	Everyone has the right to take part in the government of their country	
21.	Everyone has the right to attend meetings and join associations including Trade Unions	
22.	Everyone has the right to marry and raise a family regardless of race or religion	
23.	Everyone has the right to enjoy the cultural life of the community and to share in its scientific advancements and benefits	
24.	Everyone has the right not to be subjected to arbitrary arrest, detention or exile	
25.	Everyone has duties to the community to ensure the full recognition and respect for the rights and freedoms of others	

Adapted from *Contemporary Moral Issues* by Joe Jenkins (Published by Heinemann Educational 1997).

Workshop 2, Euthanasia

Introduction

Research the issue of euthanasia, defining key concepts such as voluntary/non-voluntary euthanasia, active and passive euthanasia. Outline the legal perspective comparing approaches in Britain with other countries including The Netherlands. Research some religious perspectives from the tradition of Christianity and/or one other world religion.

Discussion

Through discussion identify the aspects of religious teachings that have influenced the legal framework. There are then two possible routes forward. Either use poems to stimulate discussion about the right to die. The following three might form a useful collection, taken from *Stopping for Death*, edited by Carol Ann Duffy.

- *Let me Die a Youngman's Death* by Roger McGough;

- *The Suicides* by Janet Fram;

- *Reincarnation* by Sujata Bhatt.

Or, alternatively, break the pupils out into five groups to discuss the following questions. They should be prepared to present their views back to the whole group in a five-minute informal presentation at the end of the discussion period.

Group 1. Is active euthanasia (involving some intervention) better or worse than passive euthanasia (where care and treatment are withdrawn) and why?

Group 2. Assisted suicide requires the help of a doctor who provides the means of death. How acceptable is that?

Group 3. Should those in a persistent vegetative state (PVS) or prolonged coma have their lives terminated on the grounds that it is no life and their families suffer distress and financial hardship? PVS can persist for many years, and recovery is unusual after three months and 'extremely unlikely' after a year.

Group 4. Are there any circumstances in which involuntary euthanasia could be acceptable?

Group 5. What might prevent euthanasia being made legal?

IMPLICATIONS FOR CITIZENSHIP

- Pupils consider their own views and values and practise expressing their views in public.

- They are then given time to prepare arguments to either support or oppose a motion for a formal debate (see next workshop) about a person's right to die.

- They will have to elect speakers for and against a motion and divide participants into supporting teams to help prepare a debate.

Workshop 3, Debating the right to die

Introduction

Introduce pupils to the procedures and organization of a formal parliamentary style debate. Explain and allocate the roles of chairperson, timekeeper, speakers, members of the floor and judges. Give time to prepare speeches/questions from the floor for the debate.

Debate

A team of speakers propose the motion, 'This house believes that people have the right to die,' and another team opposes it. The debate is then opened to the floor for more general debate (see debating society rules in Chapter 7).

Conclusion

At the end of the debate, before the workshop concludes, the judges reach a verdict, based on an evaluation of the quality and presentation of arguments. A vote is also taken on the motion.

Other possible philosophy and belief days

There is a range of alternative subjects around which such a day may be built. These include:

- religion and the media;
- worlds of difference: a multicultural approach;
- vegetarianism and animal rights;
- civil law and the values upon which it is based;
- tolerate or convert – religion as a source of conflict.

PHILOSOPHY AND BELIEF CONFERENCE: IMPLICATIONS FOR CITIZENSHIP

- Those involved in the philosophy and belief day will learn to reflect upon and discuss the value of human life and what it means to be a person.

- They learn to distinguish between legal and moral issues relating to human rights such as the right to life and the right to die.

- They will begin to understand the influence/effect of religious beliefs (eg belief in God/life after death) on social attitudes towards matters of life and death and how some of these beliefs underpin the law of the country.

- They will take part in a formal parliamentary style debate relating to the issue of euthanasia and the right to die and in so doing learn to understand and appreciate the views of others.

- Pupils learn to empathize with the experiences of people who are denied basic human rights and make informed judgements about the rights and responsibilities of individuals towards their own life and the lives of others.

- They will consider whether there are any rights that are basic to all humans and to evaluate which might be considered the most important.

CHAPTER 9

ENVIRONMENTAL ACTION

This chapter describes a range of environmental actions actually undertaken at a school and shows how these can be used to teach citizenship. Obviously, not every school will have the facilities to re-create this work exactly but it is another example of how existing activities within a school can be used to promote greater understanding of citizenship.

The Green Team

The 'Green Team', a name chosen by members of the team, was established in the mid-1990s. It built upon work of a previous group, the 'Watch Group', which had been part of a national scheme. It has grown slowly but surely since then into an established institution within the school and has engaged in a range of environmental activities, both in school and in the local community.

Organization and rationale

The Green Team is open to all pupils and students at the school. There are five main aims of the Green Team:

- to enable pupils to carry out active conservation work in their local area;

- to encourage pupils to gain enjoyment from helping wildlife;

- to teach pupils to care for and respect wildlife;

- to visit sites of wildlife value (eg nature reserves) in their local area;

GREEN TEAM NEWSLETTER, JANUARY

Happy New Year to all of you and a big thank you for all your efforts last term!

HIGHLIGHTS LAST AUTUMN

- **Numbers** of you turning up for meetings in school have been higher than ever – well done! However, attendance at out-of-school events has been less good; do try to come to some of these events.
- Donations of **tools** have been excellent; it's now much easier to equip the large numbers of you who turn up. The donation of a motor mower should make it much easier to manage the gardens this year.
- The **scrub clearing** in Mendip garden was successful but burning it was difficult as it was so wet. However, we did manage to get it going in the end, thanks to Miss Johnston and some dead cypress!
- The school **ponds** look much better thanks to your efforts; by the summer they should look superb.
- The **quad** is continuing to improve; all that sand we added last year has made the beds easier to work with.
- Support from our **sixth form** has been excellent; long may it continue!
- **River dipping** was again successful, with quite a range of small animals caught, showing the water is not polluted.

PLANS FOR THE COMING YEAR

As you know, the **school garden restoration** continues to be our main priority. I am applying for more grant aid but there's still a great deal we can get done in the meantime. To speed the process along I've included four **garden days** in the programme, where you can turn up for all or just part of the day to help with the restoration. Birdwatchers among you should be pleased that a trip to the **Chew Valley Lake** and a **dawn chorus** are included. Don't forget the **evening talks** – especially the one in March.

REMEMBER – THE MORE YOU CAN TURN UP TO THE BETTER!

Figure 9.1 Green Team newsletter

■ to teach pupils that global conservation can only be achieved by activities at a local level.

Pupils are encouraged to take part in decision-making in all activities, at all stages, in order to develop a feeling of 'ownership' of the projects undertaken. The members of the Green Team range in age from 11–18, the majority coming from the lower age range. Currently Year 12 can and do opt to help supervise younger members, and get involved in the practical work themselves, as one of their official support activities.

Meetings are held fortnightly in school, and out of school on a less regular basis. The emphasis is usually on carrying out practical conservation/environmental activities including such things as pond clearing, wildlife gardening, tree planting and nest-box construction.

A number of sites within the school grounds are looked after including two areas of trees, a quad area (which includes several eight-foot-square flower beds and a large pond) and the large and challenging school garden.

Out-of-school activities include birdwatching, winter evening talks in conjunction with the local branch of the county Wildlife Trust (a strong and important community link), summer walks (eg to nearby hills) and trips to local nature reserves.

Green Team members are issued with a newsletter each term with a programme of events (see example opposite). Notice of Green Team meetings is printed in the school diary and all other activities and feedback about the outcomes of recent meetings are advertised in the school's weekly newsletter to parents. Parental involvement is actively encouraged and currently a small but very loyal and excellent band of parents regularly support the team in a wide range of activities.

CASE STUDY: THE SCHOOL GARDEN

Historically the garden was used for Rural Science until the demise of this subject during the late 1980s. Since then a pond has been built in the garden, which is a useful resource for science throughout the school, but the remainder of the space has gradually become overgrown and is now in urgent need of restoration. While a great deal can be achieved by the efforts of the Green Team, it is

continued overleaf

continued

clear that major work is required to restore the garden to a state which can be managed by them. This major work is the reason why we required financial support.

After much discussion, the Green Team came up with an action plan and accompanying maps, supporting quotes and pupil justifications. Two important items of major work we have completed since January 1999 were to reline the pond (which has rapidly re-colonized and is teeming with life) and to clear a large area of scrub. We have received local government grant aid and funding from our PTA, for pond restoration. We were also granted £650 from a car manufacturer as part of their 'Practical Environmental Projects' scheme. We were able to carry out the scrub clearing ourselves (thus saving £260), thanks to support from parents of the Green Team and donations of tools from members of the local community. There are considerable financial implications to achieving our ambitious plans. However, the result will be the construction of a superb conservation area, excellent for a large diversity of native wildlife, and for its study by a large number of pupils ranging in age from 5 to 18 years.

BENEFITS OF THE RESTORATION PROJECT

Our main aim is to increase biodiversity and thus benefit local wildlife. However, many people should gain from the planned restoration:

- pupils in the Green Team, their families and interested members of staff have the opportunity to become actively involved in the restoration;
- once restored the garden will be a much improved educational resource facilitating ecological and scientific study, thus benefiting teachers and pupils alike;
- other curriculum areas, eg art, technology, will be able to use the improved facility;
- pupils from the neighbouring infant and junior schools will be able to use the garden.

continued

continued

MAINTENANCE OF THE GARDEN

Once the restoration is complete, the Green Team's role will be to maintain it throughout the following years, to carry out regular surveys to assess the effects of the changes on wildlife, to identify problems and to suggest ways of improving the facility for all users, whether animal, plant or human. We are recording computerized species lists and logging other observations which will form the basis of an annual report.

ENVIRONMENTAL ACTION: IMPLICATIONS FOR CITIZENSHIP

- The whole ethos of the Green Team is to encourage pupils to think about environmental implications of human activities.

- They will begin to understand more about ecology and conservation in general.

- Pupils are encouraged to become responsible citizens who will continue to implement these ideals through adulthood.

- Participating in environmental actions of this sort, pupils become aware of the world as a global community and the political, economic, environmental and social implications of this.

- Green Team provides good opportunities for participation and responsible action.

- Members are actively encouraged to become involved in decision-making processes, to consider the implications of their decisions, to implement their decisions, and to evaluate the success (or otherwise) of their actions.

CHAPTER 10

THE BUDDY SYSTEM

Context

Within a large school it is inevitable that there will be pupils who have concerns and problems. Many of these might be directly subject related and so a solution can be arrived at through help and support from the many curriculum systems within the school. Many may be related to problems of organization or relationships and in these cases often the solutions are achieved through the pastoral support systems. However, there may still be pupils who have concerns which, for one reason or another, they may not wish to bring to the attention of a teacher or a parent. In this context peers can be an enormous support and help but sometimes something else is needed. The Buddy system is another form of support that can perhaps reach those pupils who are unable or unwilling to use a more formalized system of support.

The establishment of the Buddy system upon which this model is based started out as a very personal quest for one student. During the course of her school career she had experienced problems relating to relationships and had experienced bullying in various forms. She had developed a number of strategies for dealing with these situations and a personal tutor was helpful. Unfortunately, when this tutor left, the student was reluctant to confide in her parents and decided to do something to help future generations of pupils who may find themselves in similar situations. As she said 'You don't want anyone to go through the same as you did'.

In order to accomplish her aim, the student used procedures already available within the school to establish the Buddy system. In the sixth form there is a key skills credit system in which Year 12 and Year 13 students can gain credits by making contributions to the school. These credits also appear on UCAS or employment references. The philosophy here is quite clearly that of putting something back into Key Stages 3 and 4 for the benefit of younger pupils and to act as role models. Already included in this list were such activities as in-lesson support for pupils who have a learning or organizational problem, being attached to a tutor group, paired reading schemes and other opportunities to forge positive relationships with younger pupils and also help their learning. Within this list was the opportunity for students to suggest other ways in which they could give support. This student suggested the establishment of the Buddy system and worked with a head of year and other sixth-form staff to bring it into being.

Research was carried out in two local schools where a similar process was in place. This was a useful starting point but clearly the Buddy system has to be established within the context of the individual school.

Organization

The simplest method is to divide the planning into four parts:

- identification of pupils needing help;
- identification of student helpers;
- matching those needing help with helpers;
- training.

Identification of pupils needing help

Most of the pupils who need help can be identified by teaching staff within the school. The Special Educational Needs department can be particularly helpful in this area by bringing forward names of those pupils who would benefit from this system. Some of these pupils may already be supported by inclusion in social skills groups or already receiving in-class support. Tutors can also be instrumental in helping in this area by drawing attention to pupils they think will benefit from inclusion. At this point it must be stressed that inclusion of those who will benefit from involvement should be purely voluntary. There must be no coercion.

At some stage in the process, in the way that all in-school initiatives find themselves the proud owners of nicknames, pupils needing help became known as the 'Little Buddies'.

Identification of student helpers

The project will need to be launched and it is suggested that the best place to start is in the sixth form to identify potential helpers from Years 12 and 13. Those that express an interest and demonstrate commitment become 'Big Buddies'. Where there is no sixth form, Big Buddies will need to be drawn from Years 10 and 11.

Matching Big and Little Buddies

This can be done in a variety of ways:

- In some cases there may already be a link. Perhaps the two involved travel on the same school bus, perhaps the Big Buddy has already given support in the Little Buddy's tutor group. Perhaps the two have come into contact over some other issue such as drama productions or sport.

- In some cases the Big Buddy may have a common interest/commitment. In our example, a Big Buddy was involved with the local PHAB Club (Physically Handicapped and Able-Bodied Club) and his Little Buddy had a disability.

- In some cases a Big Buddy may have experienced the same problems as the Little Buddy.

Gender may be an issue, and a difficult one to address; in our example there was a large gender imbalance, with more girls than boys in the Big Buddy team, and this meant that we were not able to match everyone with a buddy of the same gender.

Training

There is an obvious training implication to this scheme. In some cases it may be that friendship or time together is all that is needed. In others the aim must be to instil confidence into Little Buddies so that they can, increasingly, feel able to cope with their problem(s). There is the possibility that the cares and problems of the Little Buddy can be transferred to the Big Buddy and leave the latter feeling overwhelmed and depressed.

For these reasons, in our example, an outside agency called 'Off the Record' provided the training. They are a counselling organization primarily aimed at young people and they work closely with schools. (Their Web site is to be found at www.offtherecord.demon.co.uk.) A representative of 'Off the Record' organized six hours of basic training for each Big Buddy. Attendance at these sessions was mandatory for Big Buddies and additional support was available. This training was quite lengthy and by completing it Big Buddies demonstrated their commitment to the scheme. These sessions covered issues such as confidentiality and looked at child protection situations where confidentiality might have to be breached and how this was to be dealt with.

It is likely that current Big Buddies will wish to assist with the training of their successors. They have much to offer here and their participation should be encouraged to make the training for future Big Buddies more relevant and personal through the use of real recent experiences in their own environment.

It's 'cool' to have a Buddy

As already discussed there should be no element of coercion in the Buddy system, either in the identification of Little Buddies or in the involvement of Big Buddies. There may be some concern that Little Buddies might not wish to be involved in case they might be stigmatized in some way. In our example, this has not been the case and there is a feeling that it is 'cool' to have a Big Buddy. Perhaps this is the first stage in building confidence.

Regular contact

Regular contact is essential if this support scheme is to work. A useful rule of thumb is for contact to be made with the Little Buddy once a week to ensure that all is going well. Apart from this, contact is on-going, open-ended and two-way. The Little Buddy can always make contact with his or her Big Buddy, and the Big Buddy should arrange more meetings in a week if they think this is appropriate. Contact can always be made through the registers of the Buddies involved. In this way the respective tutors are also aware of the relationship and so can keep an interested eye on the Little Buddy.

Awareness of the Buddy scheme within the school

The school management team needs to be kept informed of the progress of the scheme from the very beginning. Close involvement of the sixth-form tutors (especially at the research and planning stages), of tutors of Little Buddies and of members of the Special Educational Needs Department is also essential to the success of the scheme.

It is worth keeping the governing body aware of the scheme and it may be appropriate to provide them with a regular report. A similar report can be given to heads of year.

Involvement of other students

The work of the Buddy system may be supported by other pupils in the school, and there can be some valuable spin offs. For example media studies groups could be involved in the production of posters to publicize and promote the scheme. This could form part of their studies examining the effect of publicity. In one particular case, a student involved offered the use of Makaton as a topic at the school festival and supported some other sessions taking place (see Chapter 5).

The Buddy system has to be seen as a credible activity within the school. To those already involved, either as a Big or Little Buddy, the credibility is obvious but this is less likely to be the case for others. It is worth mentioning that the success of the Buddy system may be even more apparent the further away the participants are from the actual experience and they look back and reflect on what it has meant for them, how much they gave or were given through the process.

In order for volunteers to come forward, there has to be some form of publicity and recognition. There is the intrinsic feeling that helping and doing something is worthwhile, but a more tangible form of recognition is required to encourage others to join the scheme. Clearly there are credits to be earned and references written for later use but, in addition, certificates can be awarded by the agency used to provide the professional input and training ('Off the Record' in our example). These can be awarded at assemblies, perhaps by someone from the outside agency. You may wish to involve the local press and there are thus opportunities to raise the profile of both the helpers and the scheme. Confidentiality is important and so the Little Buddies should not be formally identified or photographed on these occasions. In our case both Big and Little Buddies were eager to be photographed and named in the press article. However, this will not always be the case. In this way new Big Buddies can be encouraged from the next year group and potential Little Buddies become aware of the scheme and the possible benefits for them.

Expansion of the Buddy system

The scheme can be expanded in a number of ways.

- A self-referral system, to allow Little Buddies to identify themselves.

- A 'drop-in' system, perhaps at a lunchtime club, when Big and Little Buddies are able to get together in an informal setting and play games or work together.

- Active recruitment of more Big Buddies – this might involve a deliberate attempt to involve more male students as Big Buddies.

- An attempt to involve others in the scheme. As described the scheme is aimed at those who perceive they have problems. There may be opportunities to work with pupils whose behaviour may cause problems for others.

- Involvement of Big Buddies in the training of their successors.

Personalizing the scheme

Each school is different with different systems in place; a Buddy scheme needs to fit the ethos of the school and meet the needs of the individual pupils. In our example, the system described above was brought about largely through the initiative of one pupil. The following may be of use when considering introducing a similar scheme in your organization:

- In an 11–16 school there would not be the impetus of the sixth form and more organization would have to be undertaken by staff. The Big Buddies could quite easily be Year 10/11 pupils as long as they have good training and support.

- Links with an outside agency are dependent on the availability of counselling or other support agencies in the local area.

- It might be that the involvement of the school's doctor, educational psychologist, school's counsellor and/or, educational welfare officer could be beneficial in the establishment of such a Buddy system.

THE BUDDY SYSTEM: IMPLICATIONS FOR CITIZENSHIP

There are many implications here, for both Big and Little Buddies.

LITTLE BUDDIES

- Little Buddies will gain an understanding of the rights and responsibilities underpinning society.

- Little Buddies are encouraged to realize that they have a right to be safe and secure in society and that there are people and systems to help them.

- They are encouraged to accept that people have differences and that these play an integral role in relationships.

- For some, especially those with relationship problems, there may be an opportunity to experience the operation of a school's anti-bullying policy or a 'no blame' approach to conflict resolution.

BIG BUDDIES

- Big Buddies should gain an understanding of human rights and responsibilities underpinning society.

- Big Buddies are encouraged to realize that they can have a part to play in instilling confidence in people in order to allow them to play a role in society.

- They work to encourage people to accept that others have differences and that these play an integral role in relationships.

BOTH GROUPS

- This is an introduction to the work of voluntary organizations and so a means of identifying voluntary groups that are ready and willing to help.

- Listening to the views of others can help in understanding why problems occur.

CHAPTER 11

OTHER WHOLE-SCHOOL ACTIVITIES

This chapter describes a range of additional ideas for whole-school or large-group activities. These activities set out to stimulate opportunities for learning about citizenship within the school. The examples quoted are essentially illustrative and have been used successfully. The principal objective is to suggest ideas that may be appropriate in the environment of each school. The opportunities are almost infinite and this list merely scratches the surface.

One of our main themes about the introduction of citizenship within a school is that it is possible, with a little thought and different emphasis, to make use of existing structures and activities to teach citizenship. Whole-school issues are particularly effective for this, not only through the actual delivery of whatever the event/performance/visit, etc might be but also in the preparation for it. We will set out some other examples. In these activities, much of the learning about citizenship will be implicit in what pupils are doing. Often this stems more from the planning and delivery than from the actual event. However, some time spent with teachers reflecting on the learning about citizenship will help to embed it.

The school production

Most schools put on a school production, be it a play, a musical or a pantomime. One of the major themes of this book is that schools already do a great deal from which citizenship can be learnt and that there does not need to be a great new effort to incorporate citizenship into the curriculum. In this section we set out the learning about citizenship that is possible from such a production.

At first sight the links between a school production and citizenship might seem tenuous. In practice, however, there are many links and many opportunities for extracting learning from the production process.

It is a difficult job to put on a school production. It can be very demanding both of energy and enthusiasm and also of time. No production will be crisis free but if the central aims are borne in mind it should be possible to concentrate on what can sometimes appear to be a very small light at the end of the tunnel. Experience has shown that the following guidelines are helpful and point up some of the learning from a citizenship perspective.

The production, rehearsal and performance process should:

- challenge the experience and ability of all those involved;

- generate interest within the school and the wider community;

- create opportunities for large numbers of pupils to be involved in stage construction, acting, providing music and design work;

- encourage all involved to reflect on their achievement, discuss problems and support each other;

- enable the cast and crew to recognize and be proud of their achievement.

During the production it is important to strike a balance between helping and supporting people through the process, and working on the production itself. There is a need to set high standards, to push the boundaries and to ensure that everyone involved is improving their skills as they go along. The experience itself can be highly significant for some participants. The discussions, communication and learning to work collaboratively bring out the best in everyone. The whole process encourages and promotes participation and responsible action and all the skills of enquiry, negotiation, formulating and expressing opinions are exercised throughout. A team that works well together can produce outstanding results.

The text

The choice of text is obviously important. There are many available scripts that can help pupils to gain knowledge and understanding about becoming informed citizens. Political, cultural and social issues can be explored through the range of characters and situations that ensure that rehearsals are filled with lively debate. Other less demanding plays and musicals can still be of value in encouraging discussion about people and their place in society. It is also possible to write or devise one's own piece of drama around an issue of interest or concern; one example, from our experience, was a collaboration with the health promotion service on HIV and AIDS. The rehearsal period began with a series of workshops for the cast before they took responsibility for the shaping of the piece. It was eventually performed in front of other local schools and at times the players had to justify and defend their choice of material.

Auditions

The nature and length of auditions will depend on the production and the level of interest from pupils. We have had examples of having to beg people to take part and of trying to select from 250 aspiring participants in *Grease*. In whichever situation, it is important to audition. Not only do you assess pupils' commitment, you also see them working with others in a slightly unfamiliar environment. Both talent and commitment are required. Pupils should be made aware of this and the need for collaboration and teamwork. A group exercise to test their ability to participate in a thoughtful, sensitive and responsible way is a good idea. Inevitably, selection will leave some disappointed but many will come back even more determined next time.

Rehearsals

Time is always at a premium. Consequently productions usually have to work to tight deadlines. In practice, this helps to focus attention, raise the pressure and the intensity of the experience for those involved. This is beneficial to learning. The style of rehearsals will depend on the style of the director but creating a group identity is vital. Most productions lend themselves to the creation of natural sub-groups whose bonding is very strong. It is powerful to invite comment and suggestions for improvement, even suggesting that pupils demonstrate briefly how they would play someone else's role. Encourage older pupils to work with younger groups on particular scenes; the results can be surprising and very rewarding for both sides. After-school and lunchtime rehearsals can be enhanced by all-day sessions at weekends. The atmosphere on these occasions is unique, very intense but great fun.

Design skills

It is a good idea to involve the design and technology department and in particular GNVQ Art and Design students. The show can be used as a project with real deadlines and the opportunity to develop designs from initial sketches into real sets, costumes and programmes that are used for the show. Pupils begin with scale models and, as the concept develops, they must delegate responsibility and manage their own time as a group to ensure that the deadlines are met. Some specialist or unusual items may necessitate negotiations with people in the community and it may be possible to exchange advertising for specific items of equipment, lighting or décor.

When rehearsing more technical aspects of the production, lighting and sound for example, it is always tempting to recruit a willing member of staff. However, with support and dedication, pupils will rise to the occasion and should be encouraged to take on the responsibility. The backstage work is as important as the action on stage to ensure a good production and the more of this that can be carried out by pupils the better.

Involving the whole school

Some people will always support productions and come to all the performances. Others may be less enthusiastic and may need encouragement to become involved. Short extracts at assemblies with accompanying descriptions of the rehearsal process are useful ways of publicizing the activity and attracting interest. Another way of combining learning with publicity for the production is to conduct class tours of the set and demonstrate the different technical elements.

Pupils are encouraged to use the microphones and sound mixers, to stand on the stage and imagine the audience. In this way they begin to become aware of the pressures facing their peers who are part of the performance.

The performance

The quality of the production almost always improves dramatically, just in time for the first night. Whether it is nerves, late-night studying of lines or just luck, concerns seem to disappear at the last minute. This is useful learning. Participants recognize the importance of trusting themselves and the rest of the team to realize the best of themselves. It is easy to panic when things go wrong, but if they are encouraged to remain calm pupils are able to react sensibly to their work and evaluate their own success. Performance over several nights enables pupils to see improvement in their performance skills and they are able to correct any earlier mistakes.

After the show

The work after the show is very important. The production dominates the cast and crew's lives for several weeks and once it is over it is important to provide time for celebration of success. Certificates of achievement can be issued while T-shirts and signed programmes make attractive souvenirs. Shows are usually recorded on video and, once these have been edited and produced, the cast and crew get together to see the recording and relive the experience.

Sharing the experience allows everyone involved, staff and pupils alike, to learn about themselves. It is surprising how quickly people grow in confidence, how well they respond to demands and how they help each other to succeed.

An evening of dance

Background

This activity is one that has been run successfully over the last four years. It is an example of an activity organized within the school that can be used to draw out significant lessons about citizenship. It is not intended to be a prescriptive model of how to conduct such an evening but as an example of what can be done.

The activity involves female pupils from Years 7 to 13 and a recent welcome addition of male pupils in Year 12. Dance is an integral part of the PE curriculum at Key Stages 3 and 4 and is compulsory for all Key Stage 3 pupils, both boys and girls. It is studied at Key Stage 4 by girls who are following GCSE and non-GCSE PE courses, as well as being a popular option in the sixth-form fitness provision.

Rationale

There are four main aims for the evening of dance, as follows:

- to encourage pupils who are interested in dance to extend this interest and expertise beyond that catered for in the PE curriculum at Key Stages 3 and 4;

- to provide an excellent evening entertainment, to celebrate success and mark the ending of the spring term;

- to encourage pupils to become involved in a wider forum outside the confines of the school;

- to encourage primary/secondary schools liaison.

Involvement

At this school dance is also an extracurricular activity that is open to all pupils at Key Stages 3 and 4. After-school dance clubs have been formed from girls in each year group from Years 7 to 13. These clubs are very popular and the level of commitment shown by both pupils and staff is high. The year group dance clubs vary in size from about 20 to 40 pupils.

What happens at the evening of dance?

The event is held at school and is the culmination of the work undertaken by pupils in the dance groups. Each group and some solo performers dance to music they have chosen for themselves. The routines vary tremendously from classical to contemporary, including Rock and Roll, Street Dance and Hip Hop. Different cultures are involved with Scottish country dancing, Arabic and Irish dancing, Salsa and Afro-Caribbean dance. The choreography for the solo performances is usually the work of the individual dancer, while the choreography for most of the groups is overseen by a member of staff. In some cases a group may do its own choreography either from choice or because it is thought that the group might benefit from doing so.

Each group is responsible for its own costumes and a tremendous variety is seen on stage. The evening of dance programme (see Figure 11.1) gives a flavour of the variety of the routines. Each year a group of male teachers performs a routine to a variety of music. This proves extremely popular. Their 'theme tune' is usually YMCA. As role models these teachers have had some success since, for the last two years, a group of male Year 12 pupils has also performed at the evening of dance to thunderous applause.

Workshops and matinee performance

Workshops and a matinee are held on the day of the evening performance. Year 6 pupils (Key Stage 2) from a local partner primary school are invited to the school. Once on site, the pupils are divided into groups of about 18 to 20 and working with members of the dance clubs (usually Year 11 pupils) produce a segment of dance based on a theme. Before the primary school pupils return to their own school, they have not only performed their new sequence on stage but have also seen a performance of the evening of dance routines.

Links with other opportunities/events within the school

There are many ways in which the evening of dance, the workshops and matinee performance link up with other aspects of school life. For example:

- The school festival (see Chapter 5) includes an activity based on dance, working with a professional dancer. The two events feed each other with interested pupils and strengthen the interest in dance in the school.

- Many of the pupils involved in the evening of dance are also involved in school drama productions which involve dancing/movement.

- The Key Stage 2 pupils who visit the school and become involved in the workshops are those who return in June the following year for their induction day at school. This prior visit may help overcome some fears before their arrival at the new school.

The work of the older pupils in providing support and encouragement to other groups mirrors the type of work that is done in the Buddy system (see Chapter 10) in which a mutual interest can be the starting point for supportive relationships to develop between pupils from different years.

Possible development of the evening of dance

- Encouraging the involvement of more male pupils. It would be good to see Key Stage 3 and 4 male pupils involved. A number of boys have been involved in roles involving dance in drama productions but this has not led to large numbers becoming more widely interested in dance. Perhaps the continued involvement of the male staff and members of the sixth form will help in time.

- Greater involvement of members of staff from outside the PE department who have an interest in this area. The Scottish country dancing and the Arabic dancing groups are overseen

EVENING OF DANCE PROGRAMME

STREET JAM
Music: **When Doves Cry** by Ginowine
Dancers: Years 9 & 10
Choreography: D Barker

I HAD THE TIME OF MY LIFE
Music: **I Had the Time of My Life** by
    B Medley and J Warnes
Dancer: J Green
Choreography: J Veale

SUNSHINE AND RAIN
Music: **Kiss the Rain** by Billie Myers
Dancers: Years 7 & 8
Choreography: D Barker

CUBAN HEELS
Music: **Salsa!** by Ray Davies
Dancers: Senior dance club
Choreography: D Barker

WHITE BOYS CAN JUMP
Music: **Larger than Life** by The Back Street Boys
Dancers: S Barlow, S Mosson, M Lyon,
    R Wheeler and D Henderson
Choreography: D Barker and dancers

CRAZY!
Music: **You Drive Me Crazy** by Britney Spears
Dancer: L Burgess
Choreography: C Grimes

ARABIAN COLOURS
Music: **Glorious** by Andreas Johnston
Dancers: Year 7
Choreography: L Gunton

FINALE

COLOURS OF THE WIND
Music: **Pocahontas**
Dancer: T Green
Choreography: P Veale

ROCKIN' AND A ROLLIN'
Music: **Rockin' Sax** by Paul Rey
Dancers: Years 9 & 10
Choreography: D Barker

IN THE JUNGLE
Music: **The Lion Sleeps Tonight** by Robert John
Dancers: Year 8
Choreography: D Barker

THE JB RHYTHM
Music: **Jungle Brothers** by The Jungle Brothers
Dancers: Senior dance club
Choreography: D Barker and dancers

LFK
Music: **Bag It Up** by Geri Halliwell
Dancers: K Davies, F Gavaghan and L Grist
Choreography: The dancers

FUNKY MUSIC
Music: **Play That Funky Music** by Wild Cherry
Dancers: Male and female senior dance club
Choreography: D Barker

DISCO FEVER
Music: **Stayin' Alive** by N'Trance
Dancers: Staff
Choreography: D Barker

Figure 11.1 Evening of dance programme

by other staff members with an interest and ability in these particular varieties of dance.

■ Extending the invitations to the matinee performance and workshops to more partner primary schools in the area. Perhaps a dance group could visit the partner primary schools.

■ Extension of extracurricular dance clubs to include Key Stage 2 pupils.

■ Investment in costumes and set designs which could be used on further occasions.

An exchange visit or foreign trip

The planning stage for a visit will probably involve ICT searches and communication. Window on the World (www.wotw.org.uk) is a database promoting international school links. The exchange activity could also involve some or all of the following activities:

- An interchange of letters between British and foreign pupils getting to know each other prior to the exchange.

- An ICT link between a British and foreign school either on e-mail or perhaps a more sophisticated three-way link, video conferencing, etc.

- A project using technology to gain an understanding of the culture(s) of the country or countries involved. This could be exploited within the school by the creation of a display to be used at open evenings, parents evenings or information evenings relating to the exchange/visit involved.

- The creation of some aspect of the culture of the school(s) to be visited, eg a café on an open evening to promote the modern languages department, with signs in various foreign languages and food and drink on sale from the countries involved.

In cases where visits/exchanges involve long journeys and staying away in hotels or hostels it is very important to ensure that partners are chosen carefully. The way in which this is done is also important:

- It encourages democracy in action, by whatever means, to ensure groups work together. This is particularly important when a coach journey involves a stop anywhere. Pupils need to look out for each other in order to ensure their safety.

- It demonstrates democracy in action to ensure that, for example, partners/groups for rooms are chosen carefully and seating arrangements on the bus are democratically decided.

- It uses group work to ensure that if essential items are needed someone is responsible for bringing them. This is perhaps particularly important on a camping trip.

A musical production

The annual carol concerts, summer concerts and other musical events don't just happen. The teamwork involved here, whether in actual performances or whole group rehearsals, small group rehearsals or in the production of solo performances, is crucially important. Then there are the other organizational details which have to be addressed which mean pupils have to be responsible, reliable and work together. Issues in which pupils can be involved in include publicity. This involves liaison with artists/the art department, the reprographics team and the finance officer simply to produce the tickets, flyers, programmes, posters and other visual material needed. It also demands skills of communication and negotiation in order that this goes ahead smoothly. It also involves setting up the venue for the event(s) and taking it down and clearing up afterwards. *Careful planning* to ensure all aspects of the task are undertaken can often be delegated to pupils who, with guidance, can accomplish these tasks; they take responsibility for it and are seen to act for the benefit of others.

Production of a year book or school book

It is possible to outsource the production of these but there are real learning opportunities to be gained from producing them in-house. In order for this to work smoothly, the process has to be well organized and many schools set up a committee to take responsibility for it. Issues to be addressed include:

- The layout and graphics of the book. This can be a daunting task and the group involved will need to liaise with the reprographics staff within the school and/or outside photographers. If outside photographers are not going to be used then strategies for seeking appropriate photographs need to be thought through.

- Setting editorial policy. If the book is to include excerpts from pupils describing their experience in the school, there will need to be a clear policy on the type of input needed.

  - *Is the tone to be formal?*

  - *Can there be 'in' jokes?*

  - *Who decides on the suitability or otherwise of the content of pupils' contributions?*

- Defining the purpose of the book.

  - *Is this to be a profit-making venture or is it designed to be a service to pupils as a memoir of their school days?*

  - *If it is to be the latter, is it designed to break even or is there a budget that will subsidize it?*

- A number of market research and budgeting issues.

Production of a school magazine

Many of the issues referred to above apply to the production of a school magazine but there are some additional ones.

- *Frequency:* how often is the magazine to be published? There are implications for market research and also questions about feasibility and the availability of time in the school's busy timetable including coursework, school exams, public exams and other major productions.

- *Content:* is this to be a serious academic magazine or something more light-hearted? Also:

  - *Can it be broad spectrum or does it need a particular identity? Who has the final editorial say on what is or is not included?*

  - *Will the articles, photographs, poems, quizzes and other pieces be contributed only by pupils?*

  - *Could ex-pupils, governors, parents, teachers and other interested adults also be invited or allowed to contribute?*

- *Liaison:* could/should such a production be linked to work going on in particular subject areas? There might be links with Key Stage 3/4 English, or Key Stage 4 business studies or with the work of an extra curricular group such as a writing group, photography club or an extension of sports reporting.

Assemblies and the involvement of pupils

The role of pupils in assemblies is one that can link in quite closely with citizenship. The school may have a policy on the use of assemblies, and the involvement of pupils requires a number of questions to be answered.

- *Who is to be involved?* Equal opportunities may be an issue. You may wish to aim for each tutor group (or form group or similar) to be involved once (or at least once) every academic year in the production of an assembly.

- *What does involvement mean?*

  - *Does it mean that everyone in the group has to take part?*

  - *Does taking part mean being visible, on stage and speaking?*

  - *Does it mean everyone has to have an involvement in some way, eg producing music, writing some of the sketch or verbal input involved, dancing, lighting, reading from a book, providing costumes, working the curtains, making scenery, producing the whole venture?*

- *Ownership:* is this wholly the remit of the group involved or is the form teacher/tutor also involved?

  - *Who decides if an issue is not suitable?*

  - *Is there a power of veto?*

- *Choosing a theme:* who does this?

  - *Is it the choice of pupils?*

  - *If so, how is the choice made?*

  - *Does it link in to some school issue, a charity week or a particular celebration, for example?*

  - *What if there is conflict over the theme?*

- *How is this resolved?*

■ *Planning and rehearsals:* when is time made available for this?

- *Is there a need to negotiate over PSHE time/tutorial time for example?*

- *What if rehearsal time needs to be at lunchtime or after school and clashes with other commitments for some or is not possible for others?*

■ *Audience:* who is to be the audience?

- *Will it be other pupils in the same year or will it be pupils from other year groups?*

- *Can parents or members of staff be invited?*

■ *Recognition:* how is the contribution of those involved to be recognized?

- *Should there be some immediate praise/comment from an appropriate member of staff, eg head of year, tutor, member of school management team?*

- *Should there be a mention in a school newsletter, some form of credit or commendation (depending upon the reward systems within the school)?*

Roles of pupils at public events

This is an ideal way of encouraging pupils to demonstrate their citizenship skills to a wider forum than the tutor group, year group or school population. Every school has a number of events when it is on show. When parents, guardians or other visitors enter a school they often want information from pupils to augment the more formal presentations and performances. Pupils can perform a variety of roles with visitors.

- Meeting and greeting parents/guardians/visitors at parents' evenings, open evenings, school productions or whilst on reception duty during the school day.

- Answering questions posed by visitors on such occasions. These could arise during the course of their meeting and greeting or a more formal information system could be introduced where pupils are placed at key points within the school underneath a sign indicating they are there to help or as an information service.

- Involvement in the induction day/evening when prospective Year 7 pupils and their parents visit the school. Who better to tell them what it is really like than pupils from Years 7 to 11? This could be provided by a series of brief talks or, more informally, by being available to answer questions.

- Working with the Parent Teacher Association carrying out a particular task such as helping to serve refreshments, modelling school uniform or other functions at parents' evenings.

- Informal entertainment throughout the course of an evening, eg a group of musicians playing intermittently or a small group of actors putting on short scenes during the evening, a group of artists at work, some mathematicians involved in mathematical games, pupils demonstrating computer programs, etc.

- Pupils taking pictures of the events of the evening or interviewing visitors as they walk around the school. The feedback gained could provide some copy for a newsletter to parents or for a school magazine. It could be used in some form of coursework or homework project or to inform future planning for similar events.

■ Under supervision of a responsible adult, pupils could help run a crèche to keep younger siblings entertained during an evening event. As with many events this would involve much planning before the evening, looking at such issues as security for the young children being looked after, suitable entertainment, strategies for dealing with young children who might become distressed, refreshments, etc.

Even more ideas in brief

- Establishing a pupil bank with a High Street bank.

- Work shadowing/work placements in school.

- Guest speakers at assemblies (members of parliament, members of the European/Scottish parliament/Welsh Assembly, local councillors, charities, police, local business leaders, etc).

- Visits to cultural museums/sites (mining/industrial heritage museums, Roman villa/baths, etc).

- Practical charity work in the community (hospital fêtes, clean up the park day, visits to nursing homes, hospices, etc).

- Involvement in national organizations and events (World Challenge, Operation Raleigh, Red Nose Day, etc).

- Sponsor a child, adopt a granny schemes.

- Theme days involving research and participation with costume, food, language, etc (Bastille day, Independence Day, Thanksgiving, Victorian day, Roman day, etc).

- Industry day with representatives from local and national organizations. This might be incorporated in a careers fair or similar event.

- Environment day with workshops (tree planting, pond clearance, recycling, visit to tip, sewage works or incineration plant, etc).

- Biology, geography, history and business studies field trips.

IMPLICATIONS FOR CITIZENSHIP

- Pupils involved gain skills, knowledge and understanding about being responsible citizens.

- They will learn to appreciate the needs of others, to work co-operatively, to communicate with a wide variety of people, to participate in community events (both within and outside the school) and they will, of necessity, learn how to act responsibly.

- They will learn about the need for mutual respect and understanding of other cultures.

- They will learn to resolve differences constructively.

PART 4

SOME EXAMPLES OF CLASS-BASED ACTIVITIES FOR TEACHING CITIZENSHIP

This final section presents a range of class-based activities for teaching citizenship for various subjects from the secondary curriculum. The activities are not intended to be comprehensive in their coverage, but rather to act as a stimulus to show the type of material that teachers can use to integrate and bring citizenship issues to life within their lessons.

The companion volume to this book, *Activities for Teaching Citizenship in Secondary Schools*, contains a wider range of activities covering the curriculum at Key Stages 3 and 4.

CHAPTER 12

CLASS-BASED ACTIVITIES

PSHE/citizenship, Key Stage 4
TITLE: Information booklet

TIME REQUIRED: Five or six lessons plus preparation

AIMS AND OBJECTIVES

- To find out about the type of people moving into the area and to identify their needs.

- To explore the local area to see which council and voluntary services are available.

- To find out what information would be useful to newcomers.

- To investigate existing guides/publications to see how they could be improved.

- To use ICT and design programs to produce a well-presented and informative booklet.

- To calculate the cost of such a booklet and investigate possible sponsors.

- To investigate methods of distributing and publicizing the booklet.

Introduction

Pupils use council publications/leaflets/charity lists, etc to establish which kinds of organizations are available in the locality. They look at existing publications and identify areas which need to be improved or added.

Discussion

Pupils decide what information needs to be included and then ask a sample of neighbours and friends to see if they agree. A group of pupils could be responsible for producing a map of the local area, perhaps taking photographs of important landmarks and features. Another group could start to investigate the cost of producing the booklet.

Development

Pupils use computers to type out lists of services and organizations and for creating cover designs. Local businesses could be approached to investigate sponsorship/advertising and ways in which they could help with the large-scale production and distribution of the booklet.

Implications/conclusions

Pupils organize the distribution of booklets to local organizations, libraries and post offices as well as new housing developments and estate agents. An evaluation exercise could be held to establish how often the booklet had been used by newcomers and whether there was a need for more/other information.

Extension activities

Booklets could be designed for groups with particular needs, ie disabled people, mothers with young children, foreign-language editions, etc.

LINKS WITH CITIZENSHIP

KNOWLEDGE AND UNDERSTANDING ABOUT BECOMING INFORMED CITIZENS

- Pupils learn about local government and other agencies and the services they provide.

- They will understand how the economy functions, including the role of business and financial services.

- They will recognize the opportunities for individuals and voluntary groups to bring about social change locally.

DEVELOPING SKILLS OF INQUIRY AND COMMUNICATION

- Pupils learn to research local issues, canvas local residents and investigate local sources of information.

- They develop reasoned arguments and courses of action from the information gained in research and to express them in class.

DEVELOPING SKILLS OF PARTICIPATION AND RESPONSIBLE ACTION

- Pupils learn to use their imagination to consider other people's experiences and think about, express, explain and evaluate what other people might want or need.

- They take part responsibly in school- and community-based activities.

- They reflect on the process of participating through evaluating the effectiveness of the work that has been done.

English/citizenship, Key Stage 4
TITLE: Charity advertising

A single (extendable) lesson examining charity advertising to explore the role of the media and the use of images and language to influence opinion.

TIME REQUIRED: One lesson, with possible development to two or three, plus preparation time

AIMS AND OBJECTIVES

For citizenship:

- To consider the work of voluntary bodies.

- To examine one role of the media.

For English:

- To consider the effect of different advertising techniques to influence opinion, including the use of emotive language and presentation.

- To raise awareness of the role of advertising.

- To prepare for reading comprehension of SATS exam.

Introduction

In this lesson, using real charity advertisements, the class will begin to understand what charities do and how their messages are transmitted. They will also begin to understand the wider role of advertising. Introduce the subject by distributing a range of adverts and leaflets from charities.

Discussion

As a whole class, discuss why charities advertise and the problems that charities have to consider in doing so (eg cost).

Take one advert (from Amnesty/NSPCC/Oxfam/RSPCA, etc) and explore the effectiveness of it considering visual impact, use of graphics and pictures, layout and language. Discuss the pros and cons of different techniques (why/why not colour/pictures/representation, etc). Then ask pupils in small, mixed ability, groups to examine and analyse a charity leaflet. They will need to read it closely to be able to do this.

Development

Ask groups to present their views back to the class as either an oral presentation or in poster form. It could be written up later as exam preparation.

Extension

In later lessons, pupils could research (including use of the Internet) a particular charitable issue in which they are interested, invent a charity and prepare an advert considering task, audience and purpose. They could write a commentary explaining their choices and considering its effectiveness.

LINKS WITH CITIZENSHIP

KNOWLEDGE AND UNDERSTANDING ABOUT BECOMING INFORMED CITIZENS

- Pupils learn about the effects advertising and the media have on public opinion and become aware how people's opinion is shaped by the use of language and images.

- They learn about the work of charities.

DEVELOPING SKILLS OF ENQUIRY AND COMMUNICATION

- Pupils learn to think about topical issues, particularly those related to charitable work.

- They learn about and develop opinions about these issues and express them in the group and in writing.

- They learn to take part effectively in class discussions.

DEVELOPING SKILLS OF PARTICIPATION AND RESPONSIBLE ACTION

- Pupils learn to examine viewpoints other than their own.

- They learn to take part responsibly in group activities.

Maths/citizenship, Key Stage 3
TITLE: House prices

A single lesson using variable house prices as a way of exploring percentages.

TIME REQUIRED: One lesson plus preparation

AIMS AND OBJECTIVES

For citizenship:

- To examine the social and community issues around the subject of increasing house prices.

For maths:

- To understand increased percentages.

Introduction

Hold a general class discussion to identify how much or how little the class knows about house prices, locations, etc. Develop the idea that comparable houses are priced differently according to the area in which they are situated.

Give each pupil a copy of the worksheet (Table 12.1) which gives an indication of the variation in prices by area. Teachers should choose an area local to their schools and will need to find this local information from newspapers or an estate agents office.

Development

Ensure the pupils understand the meaning of the figures in Table 12.1 and ask them to work on some questions, either individually or in pairs. The questions could include the following:

Table 12.1 House Prices (£) in the south-west of England

Area	1999	2000	Percentage rise
Bath and North-East Somerset	94,028		38.7
Bristol	72,837	88,593	21.6
Dorset	95,572	114,848	20.2
Gloucestershire	86,466	100,199	15.9
Herefordshire	77,375		16.9
Monmouthshire	80,964	91,417	
North Somerset	77,326	95,759	23.8
Somerset	72,788	91,092	25.1
South Gloucestershire	77,119	93,486	21.2
Swindon	72,858	89,801	
Wiltshire	93,236	115,428	23.8
South-West	79,824		20.6
England and Wales	84,973	99,295	16.8

Figures relate to average price, in pounds sterling, of residential property sales completed in January–March 2000 compared with the same quarter in 1999. Source: Land Registry.

Associated information:

- estate agents feel that house prices may have peaked;

- more and more people were seeking homes in the South-West, having left London;

- those seeking houses ranged in age from young couples to retired people and encompassed professional people and wealthy parents seeking a home for their children going to Bristol University;

- some people saw the purchase as an investment and intended to sell within a few years.

- Work out with pupils how to calculate the 38.7 per cent rise for Bath and North-East Somerset.

- Ask pupils to fill in the remaining blanks in the table.

- The percentage increase in the prices of a house might affect where you decide to live. Your bank manager/financial advisor tells you that you can borrow money to buy a house taking out a mortgage up to three times the amount that you earn. If you earn £30,000 a year, what size mortgage can you get? In which regions can you afford to buy an average-priced house this year? What about last year?

- You already have a house but you want to work out how much the value has changed as you want to sell it. If your house is in Swindon (or somewhere appropriate to your data and chart!) and it was valued at £80,000 to buy last year, what is it worth now?

- Your cousins live in a pleasant country house in Dorset, which their parents bought for £100,000 last year. How much is this house worth this year? If the predicted increase for 2001 is 15 per cent, how much will it be worth in 2001?

- You are working for the local paper and are asked to give homeowners in Bath and North-East Somerset (or wherever) information about the value of their house now compared to last year. This could be done for three other local areas. Write a few lines for the paper and conclude by giving a predicted percentage increase or decrease for next year. Show what will happen to the average price of a house in Bath and North-East Somerset as a result of this predicted increase/decrease.

LINKS WITH CITIZENSHIP

KNOWLEDGE AND UNDERSTANDING ABOUT BECOMING INFORMED CITIZENS

- Pupils learn about the significance of the media in society (in this case through the use of statistics to inform people).

- They learn about the economic, environmental and social implications of difference and interdependence across communities (in this case the ability to purchase, or not to purchase, in certain areas).

DEVELOPING SKILLS OF ENQUIRY AND COMMUNICATION

- Pupils learn to think about topical social and cultural issues and events by analysing information and its sources.

- They learn to justify orally and in writing a personal opinion about such issues.

- They learn to contribute to exploratory class discussions.

DEVELOPING SKILLS OF PARTICIPATION AND RESPONSIBLE ACTION

- Pupils learn to use their imagination to consider other people's experiences and be able to think about, express and explain views that are not their own.

Science/citizenship, Key Stage 3
TITLE: How noisy is this school?

One or two lessons on noise.

TIME REQUIRED: One or two lessons plus preparation

AIMS AND OBJECTIVES

For citizenship:

- To consider the environmental issue of noise.
- To develop acceptable solutions to resolve noise problems.

For science:

- To survey different parts of the school and to identify noise problems.

Introduction

Introduce the subject by considering the issue of noise. Discuss in the class the implications of noise in society and in this school in particular. What are the rules about noise in the school? How is this addressed in society at large? What does the law say? (Possible sources of information include the Department of the Environment, Transport and the Regions, and the Noise Abatement Society, PO Box 518, Eynsford, Dartford, DA4 0LL.)

Development

Ask pupils to work in small groups of two or three. Each group is allocated a particular site in the school that they must visit to fill in the worksheet (Table 12.2). They should use a sound meter, if one is available.

Groups report back to the class and a combined list of problems is compiled. Groups should be asked to explain why the levels of noise they have identified might be a problem and its effect on other people.

Each group should be asked to suggest solutions for the site/noise they have identified and which they have convinced the class is a problem. (Alternatively, individual pupils could write a brief report of their findings and share this with the class.)

Table 12.2 How noisy is our school?

Work with a partner or in a group of three.

Imagine you are on a committee which is preparing a report on the problems of noise in school. Your group will survey one part of the school. Ask permission before you go into a classroom/office, etc. Do the survey quickly and without disturbing anyone.

School noise survey

Place:			*Date:*
List of sounds that can be heard	*Is it noise? (yes or no)*	*Sound level (see below)*	*Notes:*

List sounds from inside and outside rooms. Assess sound levels using a sound meter or estimate the level using the following scale:

1 = VERY QUIET   2 = QUIET   3 = AVERAGE   4 = LOUD   5 = VERY LOUD

Notes should include any other relevant information including who may be affected. Use your notes as the basis of a brief report to the committee of your findings and recommendations.

LINKS WITH CITIZENSHIP

KNOWLEDGE AND UNDERSTANDING ABOUT BECOMING INFORMED CITIZENS

- Pupils learn about the legal and human rights and responsibilities underpinning society (the work should be in the context of problems/hardship caused in society by people allowing loud music, ongoing maintenance noise, etc).

- They learn about the importance of resolving conflict fairly (by identifying solutions which address the needs of all concerned).

- They learn about the political, economic, environmental and social implications of noise (EU regulations concerning noise abatement, UK noise legislation, etc).

DEVELOPING SKILLS OF ENQUIRY AND DEBATE

- Pupils learn to think about topical issues through analysing information from a wide range of sources (including the Internet) and form an opinion about the issues.

- They justify orally and in writing their personal opinion about such issues.

- They contribute to group and exploratory class discussions.

DEVELOPING SKILLS OF PARTICIPATION AND RESPONSIBLE ACTION

- Pupils learn to use their imagination to consider other people's experiences and put themselves in the others'

Geography/citizenship, Key Stage 3
TITLE: Shanty towns. Why they exist and the problems that occur in them

A single (or extendable) lesson on shanty towns and urban poverty.

TIME REQUIRED: A single lesson plus preparation – extendable to two or three lessons

AIMS AND OBJECTIVES

For citizenship:

- To understand the deprivation experienced by people because of a lack of economic, social and political opportunities.

For geography:

- To identify the location of shanty towns, both locally and globally.

- To understand who lives there, ie different ethnic divisions that occur in cities in Less Economically Developed Countries (LEDC).

- To understand the reasons for rural–urban migration including 'PUSH' and 'PULL' factors.

Introduction

This could be teacher led/brainstormed from pictures or other resources. Explain that shanty towns are mainly a phenomenon of LEDC cities. The nature of shanty towns is essentially unplanned, haphazard settlements where the poorest people and lowest social classes live. Shanty towns have grown up because of rural-to-urban migration and poverty in the countryside.

Tasks

- Watch an appropriate video, eg *Skyscrapers and Slums* (Brown, L, Producer, BBC 1980). This video, set in the *favelas* of Rio de Janeiro, is a good way to show the deprivation. The visual images will stimulate a discussion, the impact will be great. (This video will be in the BBC Broadcast Archives and as they are educational will be available for purchase, although you cannot access details on the Internet but have to contact your local BBC office for details.)

- Contrast *favelas* with the middle-class suburbs of Rio de Janeiro.

- Discuss the issue for South America. Why are the middle-class suburbs white and the *favela* inhabitants black and Amerindian?

- Other matters that could be addressed include:

  - *Genocide of street children;*

  - *Does poverty cause despair and encourage crime?*

  - *Why does inequality exist?*

  - *Why is little being done to help* favela *inhabitants?*

Development

- Look at shanty towns in other areas of the world and contrast them.

- Compare the problems of the shanty towns with the problems of inner cities in More Economically Developed Countries (MEDC).

- This could lead to an extended piece of writing for homework that could discuss one of these topics in more depth.

LINKS WITH CITIZENSHIP

KNOWLEDGE AND UNDERSTANDING ABOUT BECOMING INFORMED CITIZENS

- Pupils learn about the world as a global community and the political, economic, environmental and social implications of this.

- They learn to have an understanding of basic human rights and how these are sometimes denied.

DEVELOPING SKILLS OF ENQUIRY AND COMMUNICATION

- Pupils learn to think about topical political, cultural and social issues, problems and events by analysing information and its sources.

- They learn to form, express and justify a personal opinion about such issues, problems or events.

- They learn to contribute to group and exploratory class discussions.

DEVELOPING SKILLS OF PARTICIPATION AND RESPONSIBLE ACTION

- Pupils learn to use their imagination to consider other people's experiences.

German/citizenship, Key Stage 4
TITLE: Rules, rights and responsibilities

A single lesson dealing in German with rules, rights and responsibilities.

TIME REQUIRED: Single lesson plus preparation

RESOURCES REQUIRED: Illustrations and text of the topic to be covered. Use any suitable resources available to you. In this example we have used *Projekt Deutsch, Book 4* (Brien, Brien and Dobson, 1993).

AIMS AND OBJECTIVES

For citizenship:

- To develop awareness of rights for teenagers.

- To compare and contrast similar rights in Germany.

For German:

- To practise how to use and develop structure with modal verbs.

Background

The class has already looked at the theme of rights and responsibilities within the school structure and has already designed their own set of school rules. This has given them practice using modal verbs and structure.

Activities

- Oral practice reinforcing what is currently allowed in school. Initially there is a teacher/class question and answer session, then a pupil to pupil question and answer session in pairs and finally feedback from the pairs to the teacher.

- Jungendrechte in Deutschland. *Projekt Deutsch, Book 4*, page 112. This page contains, in German, a list of actions and identifies at what ages these are permissible in Germany. These include such things as smoking, driving a car and drinking beer or wine in a pub. It then goes on to give a list of statements, again in German, relating to the legal age limit and asks pupils to identify whether the statements are true or false. Read the page and check that the class understands the meaning. Check orally whether the class feels each rule is the same for them.

- Produce two columns in exercise books, one headed with a ✓ and one with a ✗. Write each sentence in the appropriate columns. (The ✓ column is for items that are seen the same and the ✗ column is for those that are different.) Check with questioning that everyone has the same sentences in each column.

- Homework: Take the ✗ column and adapt the sentences so that they are correct for England so that they represent 'Das Jugendgesetz in England'. If there are sentences/issues about which there is no agreement in the class, pupils could be asked to find out the real rules for next lesson. A useful resource for this would be *Young Citizen's Passport: Your guide to the law in England and Wales* by Thorpe and the Citizenship Foundation.

LINKS WITH CITIZENSHIP

KNOWLEDGE AND UNDERSTANDING ABOUT BECOMING INFORMED CITIZENS

- Pupils learn about the rights and responsibilities that relate to citizens, in this case young people in different countries.

- They learn about other countries of the European Union.

DEVELOPING SKILLS OF ENQUIRY AND COMMUNICATION

- Pupils learn how to research a social or cultural issue using information from different sources to establish relevant facts.

- They learn to contribute to group and exploratory class discussions.

Music/citizenship, Key Stage 3
TITLE: Steady beat and rhythm

A double lesson on the use of a steady rhythm.

TIME REQUIRED: A double lesson, plus preparation

AIMS AND OBJECTIVES

For citizenship:

- To practise responsible participation in a class activity which demands the delivery of feedback on the work and efforts of others.

For music:

- To enable pupils to recognize, re-create and use steady beat in their listening, performing and composing.

- To perform a simple grid composition, in more than one part, as a group.

Activity

- In a circle play a game of '*Zip-zap-boing*', ensuring that it always progresses with a steady beat (the pupils should already know what a steady beat is from a previous lesson). Anyone who is out of time is out of the game. This game is probably quite commonly used in music lessons. Pupils are defined as 'zip', 'zaps' or 'boings' and stand in a circle. Rhythms are initially created by pupils calling out 'zip', 'zap' or 'boing' in turn. The game can be extended by a caller pointing to pupils in a different order to create different rhythms.

- Draw a beat grid, eight across by two down, on the board and put spots in some of the boxes on the top line (see Figures 12.1

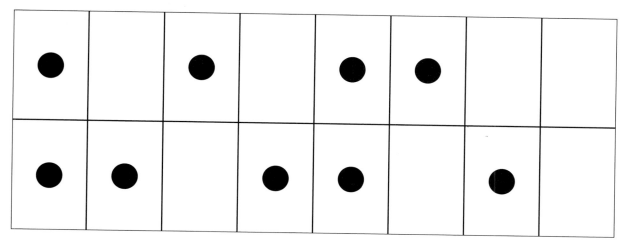

Figure 12.1 Beat grid; one of many options

and 12.2). This is, of course, one of many options.

Tapping a steady beat, inform the pupils that each box is worth one beat. Starting at the beginning they must only clap when they see a spot in the box. Make sure the class can perform this accurately without speeding up.

■ Fill in some spots on the second line and repeat the exercise.

■ Divide the class into two and ask each group to perform one line each at the same time. Swap the sides around so that they all attempt both rhythms.

■ Issue pupils with a copy of the grid to stick in their books.

■ In pairs they must compose their own rhythms in the grids and perform the two lines simultaneously at the end of the lesson. Perform using percussion.

■ As the class seems to be completing the piece, bring them together for a performance. Any who are ready early can try a 12-box long grid/performing faster/two pairs together performing four rhythms.

■ Listen to each performance and assess:

　– *Two dissimilar rhythms played accurately and with a secure steady beat at a moderate tempo.*

　– *Two similar rhythms played with a secure steady*

BEAT GRID

Figure 12.2 A beat grid

*beat at a moderate tempo. There may be some
inaccuracies.*

- *Two similar rhythms played with an awareness of
steady beat though it may be lost as the
performance progresses. Mostly accurate playing.*

- *Two rhythms played in time with themselves but
not each other. Limited awareness of steady beat
but very little.*

■ As each performance finishes encourage the class to applaud.
Give verbal feedback and ask pupils also to give feedback on
what they liked and what they did not and to give their
opinions on each performance. They should be reminded that
this could be difficult without upsetting other people. They
must choose what they say and how they say it carefully but
they must express their view. Remind pupils that everyone will
be in both roles as performer and as 'critic'.

■ Play *'Zip-zap-boing'* to finish as time allows.

Extension work

This work could be extended, specifically for citizenship, to encompass the global differences in rhythms from different cultures. The wide availability of music to all through the media has led to the fusion of different styles, and cultural and regional differences in rhythms and music are being eroded.

LINKS WITH CITIZENSHIP

KNOWLEDGE AND UNDERSTANDING ABOUT BECOMING INFORMED CITIZENS

- Pupils learn about cultural and ethnic differences in music.

DEVELOPING SKILLS OF ENQUIRY AND COMMUNICATION

- Pupils learn to form opinions about each other's work and express and justify those opinions in the group without causing offence.

DEVELOPING SKILLS OF PARTICIPATION AND RESPONSIBLE ACTION

- Pupils learn to work as a collaborative group and participation from each pupil is essential for an effective performance.

- They learn to participate responsibly. Their feedback must be reasoned and constructive. Throwaway condemnation of someone else's performance is both hurtful and unhelpful. They must also be prepared to listen to and heed the views of others.

Drama/citizenship, Key Stage 4
TITLE: Theatre as a medium for education

A series of several lessons to examine theatre as a medium for education.

TIME REQUIRED: A series of several lessons plus preparation

AIMS AND OBJECTIVES

For citizenship:

- To research a topical moral or social issue.
- To prepare a view and a message for a target audience.
- To convey that message.

For drama:

- To educate a target group through the medium of drama, having devised and performed a piece lasting approximately 20 minutes.

Introduction

- Pupils are divided into groups of four or five and asked to choose a topical issue. Topics can be self chosen or chosen from a list pre-prepared by the teacher and could encompass such issues as drug taking, AIDS, teenage pregnancy, old age, sexism, bullying, homelessness, smoking, road safety, anorexia, alcoholism, asylum seekers, drink-driving, relationships, conservation or environmental issues.

- The groups choose specific target audiences for their chosen subject, eg the elderly, primary school pupils, peers, parents/governors. Pupils must recognize the specific needs of the target audience and identify particular approaches appropriate to this audience.

- Each group needs to research their chosen topic using the Internet, CD ROMs, doctors, newspapers, teenage magazines, novels dealing with the issue, people who have experienced similar situations, surveys, books, material from charities, pressure groups, government statistical information, depending on the issue they have chosen.

- Groups need to negotiate and decide how best to use the information to devise the 'message' they wish to convey.

Development

- Each group works together on their production piece, bearing in mind the message to be conveyed (ie the 'education' for the audience) and thinking how this is to be conveyed to the target audience. They need to think about the characters they are portraying and empathize with them.

- Pupils should be encouraged to use different dramatic techniques, eg a play, a series of scenes, humorous sketches, realistic scenes, stereotypical scenes which highlight how not to behave, a series of scenes in which the central character's behaviour determines the varied outcomes, newspaper headlines or stories, monologues, freezes or tableaux, poems, OHPs, quiz shows, flash forwards (to see the outcomes or results of a particular action), audience votes, slides, dreams and nightmares, parodies of popular adverts.

The dynamics of the group and the way it promotes responsible and collaborative behaviour are hugely important here. Pupils need to work with the group, to contribute and to be involved. They will need to work with all their sensitivity, generosity, commitment and concentration. Leadership and supportive behaviour will also be important.

Performance and evaluation

- The plays/scenes/sketches are performed. The target audience is not usually there, but is not precluded from being present.

There is, however, always an audience of some sort present (usually the performers' peers) so that audience reaction can be measured.

■ The performance is evaluated for its dramatic content and effectiveness of the message conveyed.

■ Pupils are asked to evaluate their contribution to the group and the group discusses how they went about their task and what worked well and what did not. The teacher should be involved in this, adding feedback on what he or she observed during the progress of the series of lessons.

LINKS WITH CITIZENSHIP

KNOWLEDGE AND UNDERSTANDING ABOUT BECOMING INFORMED CITIZENS

- Pupils learn about the legal and human rights and responsibilities underpinning society and how they relate to citizens, including the role and operation of the criminal and civil justice systems.

- They learn about issues of democracy and representation.

- They learn about the origins and implications of the diverse national, regional, religious and ethnic identities in the United Kingdom and the need for mutual respect and understanding.

- They learn about issues of collective and individual responsibility.

DEVELOPING SKILLS OF ENQUIRY AND COMMUNICATION

- Pupils learn researching topical political, spiritual, moral, social or cultural issues, using information from different sources, including ICT-based sources.

- They form, express, justify and defend orally and in writing their personal opinions about these issues.

- They contribute to group and exploratory class discussions.

DEVELOPING SKILLS OF PARTICIPATION AND RESPONSIBLE ACTION

- Pupils learn to use their imagination to consider other people's experiences and be able to think about, express and explain views that are not their own.

- They learn to negotiate, decide and take part responsibly in group and school activities.

- They reflect on the process of participating, their role and contribution.

Design and technology/citizenship, Key Stage 3
TITLE: Technology and the quality of life

A series of lessons exploring how technology can affect the quality of life.

TIME REQUIRED: A series of up to 6 lessons over several weeks

AIMS AND OBJECTIVES

For citizenship:

- To research ways in which technology can affect the quality of life.

- To facilitate discussion and debate within the group.

For design and technology:

- To design and make an electronic device that can make life easier.

- To learn to solder and to use equipment safely.

- To construct a sensing circuit.

- To plan and make a device suitable to house the sensor.

Introduction

Ask pupils to discuss ways in which technology has helped to improve the quality of life. Prompt them to consider life at home without washing machines, electric cookers, etc. Ask them to consider how the disabled have benefited from technological advances.

Introduce the fact that they will be asked to design and make a sensing device that detects dark, light, moisture, touch or pressure. Develop the discussion to introduce the idea that there are many areas in the home that can and do use sensors to detect these. Encourage pupils to discuss situations in which a sensor might be useful, eg to think of all the times that the washing gets wet when left outside, when the heat in a room kills a plant, when lights are left on in a room which is empty or someone forgets to turn the security lights on.

Inform pupils that the device must have an 'input' (a sensor, which reacts to a particular situation, eg a light-dependent resistor which senses how much light there is in a room), a 'process' (which is an action that is prompted by the sensor, eg a switch) and an 'output' (which is what the device can do, eg make a noise, make a movement or make a bulb light up).

Development

Ask pupils to research individual home needs and find a problem to solve which will involve a real use for a sensing device. Once they have all chosen a problem ask them to make appropriate preliminary notes and sketches.

Pupils should bear in mind the need to indicate to the user the purpose of the device. For example, if the problem to be solved is that a rabbit needs to be put away when it gets dark, and the device is a dark detecting circuit which makes a noise to remind the rabbit's owner of this fact, then the 'Dark Detecting Rabbit Reminder Device' could be in the shape of a rabbit or a hutch or a carrot.

Project-making

In order for the project to succeed, pupils will need to:

- plan the order of making;
- keep a diary of all planning and the work done;
- produce ideas as a good quality drawing with notes;
- ensure that all tools are used safely;
- use tools and soldering successfully;
- concentrate on the quality and finish of the container;
- design and use a set of tests for the sensing device;
- evaluate the effectiveness of the device;
- suggest improvements for design.

LINKS WITH CITIZENSHIP

DEVELOPING SKILLS OF ENQUIRY AND COMMUNICATION

- Pupils learn to think about social issues such as disability and the use of technology.

- They learn to analyse information.

- They learn to express a personal opinion and justify it, and contribute to exploratory class discussions.

DEVELOPING SKILLS OF PARTICIPATION AND RESPONSIBLE ACTION

- Pupils learn to use their imagination in considering other people's experiences.

- They reflect on the process of participating.

- They use tools and techniques safely and responsibly.

FURTHER READING

Brien, A, Brien, S and Dobson, S (1993) *Projekt Deutsch, Book 4*, Oxford University Press, Oxford

Brown, L (producer) (1980) *Skyscrapers and Slums*, BBC Television, London

Duffy, CA, ed (1996) *Stopping for Death*, Viking Poetry (Penguin), London

English Speaking Union (1999) *Pros and Cons*, Routledge, London

Jenkins, J (1997) *Contemporary Moral Issues*, Heinemann Educational, London

Keenan, B (1993) *An Evil Cradling*, Vintage, London

Phillips, J and Hooke, J (1998) *The Sport of Debating: Winning skills and strategies*, University of New South Wales

QCA/DfEE (1998) *Education for Citizenship and the Teaching of Democracy in Schools* (The Crick Report), QCA, Sudbury

QCA/DfEE (1999a) *Citizenship: The National Curriculum for England Key Stages 3–4*, QCA, Sudbury

Thorpe, T and the Citizenship Foundation (2000) *Young Citizen's Passport: Your guide to the law in England and Wales*, Hodder and Stoughton, London

For citizenship

QCA/DfEE (1999b) *Preparing for Working Life*, QCA, Sudbury

QCA/DfEE (2000) *Citizenship at KS3 and KS4: Initial guidance for schools*, QCA, Sudbury

For euthanasia

Kennedy, Ludovic (1990) *Euthanasia: The Good Death*, Chatto & Windus, London

Age Concern, Institute of Gerontology and Centre for Medical Law and Ethics (1988) *The Living Will: consent to treatment at the end of life*, King's College, London

USEFUL CONTACTS

BBC www.bbc.co.uk/education BBC Online with linked access to a range of educational Web sites.

British Education and Communications Technology Agency, Virtual Teacher Centre Web site vtc.ngfl.gov.uk/vtc/library/pub.html is a huge resource for teachers on a wide range of subjects.

Citizen 21 www.citizen21.org.uk is an online resource for citizenship from which resources can be downloaded.

Citizenship Foundation www.citfou.org.uk is a charity supporting citizenship education.

Community Service Volunteers. This organization works with schools and colleges to enable young people to become active citizens through practical projects addressing community needs. www.csv.org.uk

The Council for Education in World Citizenship is an independent educational organization specializing in creating partnerships with local, national and global organizations to develop active learning opportunities in citizenship. www.cewc.org.uk

DfEE Department for Education and Employment. Sanctuary Buildings, Great Smith Street, London SW1P 3BT.

EU. The main European Union Web site is at http://europa.eu.int

EU. http://www.eun.org offers a civics section in its 'Virtual School' with a discussion forum and occasional contacts with MEPs

Foreign and Commonwealth Office site www.fco.gov.uk with information on studying overseas cultures.

Foreign and Commonwealth Office site www.charter88.org.uk is a contact for the campaign for a modern and fair democracy in the UK.

The Hansard Society promotes knowledge about parliament and government. It can provide high quality material for mock elections in schools. www.hansard-society.org.uk

The Institute for Citizenship. The institute's aim is to promote citizenship by developing innovative projects for citizenship education. www.citizen.org.uk

National Curriculum Web site. www.nc.uk.net

NISS www.NISS.ac.uk/world/schools.html provides a huge collated list of sources of information for schools.

One World www.oneworld.org is an organization dedicated to promoting human rights and sustainable development.

QCA. Qualifications and Curriculum Authority, 29 Bolton Street, London, W1Y 7PD.

UK Government. The Government Information Service can be found on http://open.gov.uk

United Nations Association of the UK www.una-uk.org is a source of information about Model United Nations debates.

Windows on the World at www.wotw.org.uk is an organization promoting international school links.

World newspapers www.webwombat.com provides details of how to contact over 10,000 worldwide newspapers for up-to-the-minute comment on events

INDEX